BIG MIKE, UNCLE DAN AND ME

HOW I BEAT 20TH CENTURY NEW YORK STATE'S MOST CORRUPT POLITICAL MACHINE

BY PAUL VAN BUSKIRK, PhD, AUTHOR,
and Whitney M. Fishburn, Collaborator

Machine Politics, Intrigue, Violence, and
Class Struggle in Small Town America

*"I think that, as life is action and passion, it is required of a
man that he should share the passion and action of his time
at peril of being judged not to have lived."*

—Oliver Wendell Holmes, Jr., Associate Justice of the
Supreme Court of the United States

BookBaby, Pennsauken, NJ

Print ISBN: 978-1-09830-798-1

eBook ISBN: 978-1-09830-799-8

Printed in the United States of America on SFI Certified paper.

First Edition

DEDICATION

This book is dedicated to the people of Cohoes, who supported our reform movement, volunteered their time, and donated money to challenge an entrenched political machine, knowing they may be subject to reprisals. They then stayed with their principals of reform, were mobilized to participate in their government and received national recognition for their achievements, and made this book possible.

CONTENTS

PROLOGUE

SPRING 1945

The first time I encountered Big Mike was in his restaurant, Smith's. It was 1945. My mother had promised to take me there for lunch as a reward for doing my winter chores and my spring cleanup of the yard. This was a real treat for a ten-year-old: not just going out to eat, but going to Smith's, the place in our little upstate New York town where the politicians, businessmen, and other important people went to eat, drink, socialize, and talk politics.

My mother made me dress in my finest trousers, button-down shirt, and pullover sweater. It was still cold, even though it was spring. We walked from our house on the hill in the fifth ward down to Remsen Street in the heart of the main business district. There were the five and dime stores where my mother would occasionally buy things. There was the enormous fortress-like stone building that was City Hall, Mr. Stone's Tailor Shop, Healey's Ice Cream Parlor, the new Cohoes Theater with air-conditioning, and Shahen's fruit market. It was my universe.

We would have driven downtown, but my father had left our family the year before and taken the car and our gas rationing coupons with him. I never saw him again.

Smith's, a three-story Tudor building with the restaurant on the ground floor and an apartment on each floor above, still operates today in the City of Cohoes. Back then, it doubled as the headquarters of the local Democratic Party.

Upon entering, one is met with a fifty-foot-long mahogany bar. Originally a fixture in Tammany Hall in Manhattan, once the headquarters of New York's most corrupt political machine, the bar is said to be the longest in upstate New York.

That day, the barroom was bustling. My mother and I walked the length of it to enter the restaurant in the back. Two blue-and-white Chinese vases, much taller than I was then, and maybe am now, towered over the ends of the bar. The mounted head of a moose peered down from the wall at the entrance to the dining room.

The waitress seated us at a corner table to the left of the over-sized stone fireplace. I sat with my back to the wall so I could see the action, as people-watching is one of my favorite pastimes. My mother discreetly pointed to a large gentleman dressed in a white suit, with his collar buttoned all the way to the top. He was enormous, probably about 300 pounds. He sat alone opposite us, also at a corner table. He was holding a menu but looking around the room.

"See that man? He's a political boss," my mother said in a low voice. "His name is Mike Smith."

Years later, I realized that on that day, I had seen Big Mike in his restaurant; he had recently been indicted by a special grand jury for committing election fraud and fixing property assessments, under Governor Thomas E. Dewey. Big Mike was eighty-four years old at the time. About four years later, on New Year's Eve, 1949, he passed away.

I was interested and had to ask my mother what a political boss was. She explained that he controlled the city's government, the police, the firemen, and the town leaders, including those leading our schools. I was aware that in our predominately Catholic city, mine was considered one of "the godless schools." The Catholic kids in my neighborhood told me that they could not be my friend because their priest had said that if they played with a Protestant like me, they would go to Hell. Catholic girls in town were told by their church leaders that if they kissed a Protestant boy, they would get pregnant.

Sitting with my mother, the two of us furtively regarding this enormous man across the room, I pictured my elementary school. During air raid drills, we kids would joke that if a plane ever flew over Cohoes, our school would collapse on us. We had no cafeteria, no playground, no recreation facilities—just a dirt yard and a washroom. Behind our school was a ravine where the city dumped its garbage.

I looked at him, this political boss. He reminded me of Sidney Greenstreet, the actor who played sinister characters in Humphrey Bogart movies like Casablanca and The Maltese Falcon. I asked my mother if Mike Smith had anything to do with the way our school was. Of course, she said. He ran the city's government.

As a ten-year-old, I was puzzled: How could anyone in charge want kids to live like that? I thought he probably wasn't that great of a boss.

As if he knew what I was thinking, Big Mike turned to look at me, for what seemed like minutes, resembling a stern schoolmaster. I looked away. "He is reading his menu upside down," I told my mother.

INTRODUCTION

THE "QUIET RIOT" OF 1963

Fast forward eighteen years from when I first saw Big Mike: it was about midnight on Election Day when I got word that Cohoes Mayor Santspree had called in state troopers, reporting incidents of vandalism—the shredding and burning of American flags, the ripping up of the tops of convertibles. Lives were being put at stake. Oh, Christ, here we go, I thought.

I left the celebration at St. Michael's Pavilion on Page Avenue and headed over to the police department, with its arched stone entryway and black Colonial era light hanging overhead. There was a New York state trooper standing around. The desk sergeant said they'd been getting a lot of calls about dangerous conditions. I asked, "How many calls, what kind of danger?" Five calls, he reported. "Noise complaints."

I turned to the trooper. "Have you driven through town?"

"The town's really quiet," he said, adding that he was leaving.

"I'm leaving," I said.

The next day, *The Troy Record* reported that overnight there had been a wild street parade. Somehow the Associated Press turned the story into one about a dangerous riot. I guess the AP reporter didn't talk to the state trooper. The story that ran on their national wire service was one of Cohoes out of control. The truth was more like jubilation and disbelief, as though an underdog but favorite hometown team had taken top prize. There had been noise, but no damage.

The occasion for the unrest, however it was characterized, was the sweeping win of the Citizens Party in Cohoes: after four decades of a Democratic dictatorship, the citizens of our city in upstate New York had voted for a resounding change.

Earlier that night, as the election returns came in and the tote board displayed the tallies, it was so crowded that I couldn't get to the stage where our new mayor, Dr. Jay McDonald, a beloved physician in Cohoes, stood waving and smiling before the throng of cheering Citizens Party supporters. Reporters who later told me they didn't understand how they also had not seen our victory coming were jammed among the roaring crowd.

The actual way we got it done is only part of the story. Politics is ugly, and for members of the Machine, a political party with an authoritarian leader, it was rule or ruin. It was a war between the political power players and the political reformers. The shifting loyalties, priorities, and tactics of the soldiers on either side, however, meant that ousting the Democrats had only unleashed still more intrigue: each side had factions that harbored sympathies for the other.

Fifty years later, I ask myself why I would want to write this book. The answer is that even though the local papers ran many stories about what happened after we took office, the inside story about our party's rise and fall has largely gone untold: the attempted murder of my son and me, the back room deals to try to reinstate members of the political machine, the weak party leadership after tragedy struck, the fraud and embezzlement by a key reformer, members of an incompetent press corps with Watergate-fever who went after non-stories, but missed the real ones that were fueled by hate and betrayal. They never told our side of the story. I want to fill in those gaps. There was wide community participation and support, but there was also continuous political warfare, both external and internal.

I also want to give some practical advice. If there are citizens who want to overthrow bad leaders and restore their Constitutional freedoms, they might not know how to do it. They might not know how to overcome the apathy that takes root when bad leaders stay in power for too long. We developed a system for doing these things and didn't deviate from it. That's how we did what everybody said couldn't be accomplished. Even the former New York State Governor Thomas Dewey, with all his resources, said you couldn't beat this Machine. We did that, and more!

PART ONE: REVOLUTION

CHAPTER ONE

SITE OF THE FALLING CANOE

The area between the Adirondacks and the Catskill Mountains in upstate New York, the City of Cohoes is divided roughly into thirds: the Western plain plateau, the river plain, and Van Schaick Island, the fat finger of land near where the Mohawk River empties itself into the Hudson River from 170 feet above. The Cohoes Falls are generally accepted as the source of the city's unusual sounding name. According to one story, "Cohoes" was a Dutch attempt at "ga-ha-oose," the Mohawk word for "falling canoe."

Even though Niagara Falls is only slightly larger than Cohoes Falls, the latter's potential to draw tourists interested in nature's more dramatic side seems to have escaped the notice of the public. The estimated number of tourists to visit Niagara Falls annually is about twenty-eight million people. In Cohoes, it's nil.

However, the falls in Cohoes—among the largest east of the Rocky Mountains—has been the site of some dramatic feats of engineering. The first of these occurred during the American Revolutionary War when a Polish patriot designed and oversaw the construction of breastworks on Peebles Island, just north of Van Schaick Island, a worthy defense against the British crossing the only ford on the two rivers for many miles, as these bulwarks played an important part in the strategy for the Battle of Saratoga, the turning point of the war. Two hundred and thirty years later, these earthen structures remain largely intact.

Superb engineering also featured in the construction of the single lock system of the Erie Canal along the long, narrow

Hudson–Mohawk River plain in 1817. This nearly 400-mile-long system of locks trapped water at one level and then released it again at a lower or higher level so that barges atop the water could make their way around geographical challenges. Ultimately, barges traveling along the canal ascended and descended 675 feet of water.

Of eighty-three locks, nineteen were constructed specifically to circumnavigate the Cohoes Falls, making it possible to connect Buffalo and the Great Lakes with New York Harbor. In 1836, when the canal was enlarged with double locks, the route remained mostly the same, with eleven locks in Cohoes. To this day, several of the Cohoes locks are in good condition, monuments to this historical engineering wonder. With the completion of the Champlain Canal that ran from Cohoes north to the St. Lawrence River, by 1823 the city had become a major transportation hub for supplies and people.

Its situation along the rivers also meant that beginning in 1831, when the Erie shipping canals were at the height of operation, Cohoes was a key player in the industrial revolution. By 1870, the city's Harmony Mills were the largest water-powered cotton mills in the world, earning Cohoes the name "Spindle City." Then a series of water-power canals were constructed above and below the falls, driving vertical turbine power in the mills built between the canals. The city's population surged as mill workers arrived from French Canada, Ireland, Italy, and Eastern Europe, and were housed in hundreds of red brick row houses.

"Big Mike" Smith was among those whose parents emigrated from Ireland and found work in the mills in the 1860s. Big Mike was born on July 8, 1862, in Waterford, New York—not Ireland, as he liked to imply—just across the Mohawk River from Cohoes. When he was eight, his parents moved with him, his three brothers, and two sisters across the river to the Cohoes First Ward, into a Harmony Mills housing unit near an elementary school.

Mill workers and their families lived in well-constructed tenement homes, or in boarding houses if they were unmarried women. There were company stores for basic goods, a clinic, a volunteer fire company, and even a day care center. The mill's operator, Garner & Company, also maintained the streets, and, as the largest landlord in Cohoes, had a corps of maintenance staff, including plumbers, masons, and mechanics. For those who'd known poverty, uncertainty, and abysmal working conditions back in "the old country," it was an easy equation: stable pay, food, and shelter in exchange for loyalty and labor.

At the turn of the twentieth century, however, the mills were in distress, faltering under the pressure and competition of cheaper labor, power, and materials further south. Around that time, Big Mike, who'd once been a millworker and a lock tender, began running a saloon, right in the center of Harmony Mills housing and the Cohoes section of the Erie Canal. The saloon hosted clam steams, sponsored athletic teams, and became the hub for neighborhood news.

When the mills went belly-up, a power vacuum emerged that Big Mike would soon fill. He became the man to know if you needed a favor or wanted a job, a loan, a bucket of coal, or even a home. In return, you gave him your loyalty and your vote. People who were hit hard by the Depression figured this was a fair trade. Families in Cohoes that had once relied on the mills increasingly looked to a strongman like Big Mike for help and cover. In a sense, he became the new boss in town.

He was not the first political boss in our little city. You could say that European-style political patronage systems in America began in Cohoes. Around 1630, Dutch diamond and pearl merchant Kiliaen van Rensselaer paced off as his own an area at the confluence of the Mohawk and Hudson. The parcel was part of the original patroon that today is essentially the entire Albany Capitol

District. Rensselaer's bit of land marked by the rivers was approximately three miles wide and three miles long, and today marks the city of Cohoes. The Dutchman eventually sold off tracts to newcomers, keeping the area below the falls for himself.

The Dutch patroons in the Hudson River Valley had chartered rights to create civil and criminal courts, appoint local officials, and hold land in perpetuity. In return for these inducements, the patroon had to grow the manor's population in increments of fifty every four years. Colonists were exempt from taxes for the first ten years they lived on the manor but were obligated to pay rent to the patroon, who often oversaw the creation of the manor's infrastructure. Another way to say it is that the word of the patroon—what we'd call in English the patron—was law. Despite the passage of 200 years and a war fought against the British to end authoritarian rule, Cohoes steadfastly remained true to its patronage roots.

The textile manufacturing industry never recovered in Cohoes, and by 1960, the unemployment rate among men in Cohoes was still roughly 8.5%. The median family income was $5,573, although more than 15% of families lived on only about $3,000 a year. In today's economy, that would be about $25,000. Also at that time, a third of Cohoesiers twenty-five years and older had less than eight years of education; for the other two-thirds of adults, just less than nine years was the average. According to the same year's census, about a fifth of the couples in town were separated, widowed, or divorced, circumstances which often equated to either an onset or a deepening of poverty. Lastly, at least a third of the Cohoes citizenry was of foreign stock from French Canada, Ireland, Italy, Poland, Russia, and Ukraine.

This meant that more than a third of the Cohoes population in 1960 was relatively poor, foreign-born, uneducated, and raised according to the strict, authoritarian doctrine of a pre-Vatican II Catholic Church. That's another way to say that for at least a third of Cohoesiers, fighting for individual rights using democratic processes was neither reflexive nor, given the demands of surviving day-to-day, a priority.

The effect on the town was that in place of the mills, Big Mike's patronage system was a way to survive. His variation on a theme of Robin Hood—one for you, ten for me, but always with a wink and smile—bridged ethnic differences among the poor in town without alienating the powerful Catholic Church, with which he made sure to stress the common value of charity. To be Catholic in Cohoes also meant you were a Democrat, one of Big Mike's own.

The Big Mike brand was so entrenched that more than a decade after his death, challenging his Democratic Party inheritors to stop pocketing the profits of patronage and do something about the crumbling infrastructure, rates of unemployment, slum living conditions, and overall despair would have been unthinkable to a population where religion, ethnicity, and political affiliation had grown inseparable. It was thought better to suffer the devil you knew rather than risk being exiled for asking for more.

U.S. Speaker of the House Thomas "Tip" O'Neill once said, "All politics is local." In Cohoes, all local politics is centered in the wards which are subdivisions where voters elect representatives for various city and county offices. There are six wards in Cohoes. Especially in lower wards One, Two, and Three, the social and political lives of residents centered around their respective ethnic churches and schools, which often taught students both in English and in their native languages: French, Polish, Ukrainian, and Russian.

Big Mike had lived in the primarily Irish First Ward. Southeast of the First Ward, bordering the eastern branch of the Mohawk, was the Second Ward, home of Cohoes's oldest business district on Remsen Street. The largest ethnic groups there were Poles and Ukrainians. South of these neighborhoods was the more centrally located Third Ward, home of the larger, busier business district, which was predominately French Canadian. In 1960, these three lower wards hadn't elected a Republican since the 1930s.

In 1960, residents of the Fourth Ward, located in the southwest part of the city, did not have a dominant ethnicity, and the socioeconomic mix skewed toward middle-income levels. This ward was more receptive to Republicans, having elected one to the city council in 1947. With the right pressure applied, it was possible the Fourth could vote Republican again. The more Protestant Fifth Ward sat uphill, above the river plain. It has traditionally been the largest and most affluent ward. In 1960, it was the ward with the best chance for Republicans to win. Finally, the Sixth Ward on Van Schaick Island was home to the mostly Italian-Catholic population and the middle class. It was further from Big Mike's epicenter, and Republicans were less hated than in the lower river plain.

This establishes the political setting of this upstate community that Big Mike's Machine ruled for forty years, chronicling the town's social and economic evolution. The mill owners, Big Mike, and the Catholic Church: all were authoritarian institutions suppressing challenges to their authority and the apathy this created. Big Mike parlayed his political chips with Dan O'Connell, Albany County Democrat leader, to create one of the nation's most powerful and corrupt political machines that were designed to be invincible.

CHAPTER TWO

THE POLITICAL MACHINE THAT UNCLE DAN AND BIG MIKE BUILT

Big Mike's chauffeur was found murdered in a house of ill repute across the river in Troy. At the age of eighty-four, Big Mike was indicted by New York Governor Dewey for tax assessment conspiracy and for being an accessory to false voter registration. Friend and political associate President Franklin Delano Roosevelt, whom he supported as a delegate both for governor and president, once ordered the presidential train to make an unscheduled stop in Cohoes so that he could shake hands with his old friend: Big Mike Smith.

For many Cohoesiers, their revered and adored patriarch Big Mike was viewed as the man in town who would reliably do whatever he could to lend a hand. I think he genuinely liked people and enjoyed helping them, but what he did, he also did for the sake of his power, to keep his political machine running.

Frank Robinson's book *Machine Politics: A Study of Albany's O'Connells* describes political machines as having the same key components. An authoritarian "boss" controls the party workers and selects the elected officials to run for the functions of the local, county, or state governments. This boss has sway over legislative policies and municipal hiring and firing and awards quid pro quo city contracts. Protection from violence or other "mishaps" is usually assured by kickbacks, typically called "donations to the party," from vendors and city workers in patronage jobs, including in city courts and police departments, which often rely on brutality to control poorer neighborhoods. City ward healers chosen by the boss are responsible for getting out the vote and handing out patronage jobs and other favors. The kickbacks and party donations are typically used to buy votes and support the boss, the organization, and, on occasion, the party committee members.

Political bosses, according to Robinson, like to keep taxes low so they remain in favor, but that means that municipal services are also kept to a minimum. For example, one winter, when my neighbors complained about the especially heavy snow that was never plowed, making the roads impassable, a city official told them, "God put the snow there, and God will take it away."

The low taxation and low level of municipal services like those I grew up with in Cohoes also equate to poor public school facilities. Most of our elementary schools were built in the 1870s and have been poorly maintained since then. Political bosses appoint all the members of a school board rather than having the slots open to election. A referendum was required for an elected school board, and only the city common council could approve a referendum.

Big Mike himself probably only completed primary school, since mill workers' children typically did not go to high school, instead working in the mills twelve hours a day, six days a week, for seventy-five cents a day. So, it's possible Big Mike could neither read nor write, but I don't think that is true. I believe he just wanted to poke a finger in the eye of the elitist Albany County Republicans, taunting them with the message, "You think you are so smart, but even an illiterate can beat you at your game."

In 1886, a decade before he started running the saloon, Big Mike got a job through politics as a lock tender at lock #18 on the Erie Canal, overlooking the Cohoes Falls. It was his first experience with politicians, since this patronage went through the local

Democratic organization. Today, you can stand on the wall of this lock, as Big Mike once did.

In 1895, he parlayed his local support into a seat on the elected board of Albany County supervisors. He was the only Democrat to win one of the six seats in Cohoes. In 1911, he was elected the Democratic Party commissioner of elections by the Albany County legislature, where he learned about election laws, particularly for primaries. By now, he had perfected the art of exchanging patronage for votes.

For years the City of Albany and the County had been ruled by a corrupt Republican political machine. In 1919, when Dan O'Connell ran as a reformer for city assessor and won, he was the sole Democrat elected in Albany that year.

O'Connell took over control of the Albany County Democratic Party in 1921 with the support of Big Mike's committeemen's vote. Talking about their big wins in Albany and Cohoes in 1921, Dan O'Connell said, "Mike and I put this thing together." They now controlled the life blood of their political organizations, patronage.

By 1923, Democrats outnumbered the enrolled Republicans for the first time in Cohoes, and the next year, Big Mike was elected as a state committeeman.

Throughout the next decade, similar power struggles continued, primarily with a resurgent Republican Party that even tried cross-endorsements with other Democrats, but Big Mike stayed on top until his death in 1949.

One reason for Big Mike's dominance during the 1930s was the Great Depression. The country's hard times meant good times for Big Mike, who could now dispense patronage from the city, state, and federal government. He oversaw the local patronage of more than 700 jobs available through his friend, the President Franklin D. Roosevelt's Depression-era Works Progress Administration, which expanded his influence in the community.

The O'Connell Machine operated in much the same way as Big Mike Smith's. However, O'Connell made deals with Republicans to cross-endorse candidates for State Supreme Court Justices, which gave him the four judges he would need to counter any legal action brought against his own or Big Mike's Machine.

Dan O'Connell designed his empire to be invincible. He knew that if he had the district attorney's office in his corner, none of his people would be indicted. If he was attacked from the outside, he could count on his judges to reverse any actions taken against him or tie them up in the court for years. In addition to his own influence, with the protection of Dan O'Connell, Big Mike Smith was essentially immune.

When Governor Dewey was elected, one of his promises was to break the back of the O'Connell and Smith Machines. As district attorney in Manhattan, he had broken the back of Tammany Hall and sent its leaders to jail. Dewey appointed a special prosecutor and indicted Big Mike and twelve of his minions, one of whom had voted seven times. Dan had his judges tied Dewey up in court for two years. Dewey was getting ready to run for president and wanted the investigation behind him. Walter Wertime Jr., Cohoes's Republican Leader, wanted Dewey to keep the charges against Big Mike; Dewey refused. Dewey and O'Connell settled: thirty-three persons pleaded guilty to misdemeanors, with twenty-five getting suspended sentences and eight serving short jail sentences ranging from two months to a year. Dewey summed it up by saying, "The Tammany Hall Machine braves are pikers compared to this [O'Connell's and Big Mike's] machine" according to Frank Robinson in his book, "*Machine Politics.*"

On the day of Big Mike's funeral, all of the schools in town closed, probably so teachers could attend the service, but also to show respect for the city's favorite boss.

More than sixty years after Big Mike's death, a Cohoesier wrote a piece in memoriam, fondly recalling as fact a tall tale I often heard used to prove Big Mike's grand humanity. The story goes that even though Native Americans were not given the right to vote until 1934, as the op-ed author wrote, "affirmation came earlier in Cohoes by Smith's decision." That's because Big Mike saw a Native American man milling around a polling station, unable to vote because it was still illegal for him as a non-White to do so. Big Mike is said to have told him that his vote should count and ushered him inside. I think it proves less Big Mike's magnanimity than his tendency to circumvent the law for his own benefit. When your word is law, a vote is a vote, and everybody wins.

Big Mike's house, referred to as the "Big House." (circa 2018) near the mill housing in his beloved first ward. With its many garages in which housed his Rolls-
Royce, Packard and a bus converted to a campaign wagon that Cohoesiers called
his "land yacht."

On the left, Big Mike with his 10-gallon hat and cigar, congratulating Mayor
Roulier, on the right, being elected in November 1939. Roulier served as Mayor
for twenty years and the Democrats used this photo in their campaign literature
to demonstrate that the Machine was invincible.

The first time I encountered "Big Mike" was when I was a 10 year old child having lunch with my mother in his restaurant called "Smith's" with the 50 foot long mahogany bar, originally a fixture in Tammany Hall. My mother told me he was a "political boss" and controlled everything. Little did I know the role I would play in my community's political machine or did I?

The Harmony Mills were said to be the largest water power cotton mills in the world. They are listed as the Harmony Mills Historic District on the National Register of Historic Places. This picture shows Harmony Mill No. 3 today which was renovated in 2005 for upscale residential units. Big Mike along with some of his six siblings worked in the mills for 75 cents a day.

CHAPTER THREE

THE INHERITOR

During the 1950s, the Machine was led by Warren Smith, Big Mike's nephew, and the Republicans in town had not managed to weaken Big Mike's Machine. In fact, it would soon become apparent that Big Mike's Machine was at its apogee—that is until 1959, when with a citywide election coming up, when Warren Smith stepped down as the leader of the machine Big Mike had built, citing health concerns (perhaps aggravated by an ongoing IRS investigation into his taxes). With a citywide election coming up, his younger cousin and heir apparent, William J. Dawson, still would need to secure his mantle as head of the party.

Many in town considered Bill Dawson to be a good family man. He was handsome, with a strong jaw and chiseled features, although he stood only about five-feet-one-inch tall. When he was about ten years old, Dawson fell from a tree, or so the story goes. The accident was said to have left him with spinal injuries that stunted his growth.

Dawson was born on July 1, 1918, the year before the last Republican mayor in his lifetime was elected in Cohoes. Although I was born seventeen years later, we both grew up under Democratic Party rule and both had uncles who were political bigwigs in town. Walter Wertime, a prominent lawyer and the Chairman of the Cohoes Republican Committee, was one of my mother's brothers. My uncles Walter and George didn't have much to do with us. My mother, a Socialist who didn't attend church, didn't seem to care one way or another. I never spoke with my Uncle Walter until well into my adulthood, nor did I communicate much with my maternal grandparents.

Bill Dawson's home environment would have been different than mine. His uncle, Dennis Dawson, was a law clerk with my grandfather and uncle's firm, rising through the ranks in the Democratic Party from Cohoes corporation counsel and police court justice, eventually becoming the attorney for Albany County.

Since Bill Dawson's maternal grandmother was Big Mike's sister, his family would have been steeped in the idea that family, Catholicism, and voting for the Democratic Machine were all one and the same: if you disagreed with one, then you disagreed with all. Growing up in that environment, raising the property assessment on your political enemies was sanctified.

It would have been normal in the Dawson and Smith families to think that city workers and teachers should pay an annual monetary tribute for having their jobs. Dawson's own family enjoyed the fruits of nepotism: his father was a foreman at the city's water department pump house. For a short time at least, the family lived above the pump house on North Mohawk Street. In time, Dawson's father became commissioner of public works. At one point, there were at least ten Smith–Dawson family members on the city payroll.

It made sense that Dawson's family members were accustomed to thinking that being in power was their right, and they wouldn't have given much thought to whether that was right or wrong. Things just were what they were. Once his cousin Warren handed him the reins, Bill Dawson set up shop at the Elks Club, where he required all city vendors to pick up their checks after leaving their "donation" to the Party.

He was haughty, and not a journeyman politician, which many rank and file Democrats resented. At forty one, Bill Dawson had neither been a ward healer nor done any significant party organizing. His greatest talent was being the only electable relative of

Mike Smith, so the party unanimously elected him chairman, citing his experience and credentials, without specifying what they were exactly.

Dawson was a commercial artist and an editorial cartoonist for *The Troy Record*. He also ran a private detective agency, but he was a lesser businessman than his Great Uncle Mike had been when it came to running the Machine. With Big Mike, if you didn't pay the expected 10% kickback, you didn't get hired for a job, or the city didn't purchase equipment from you next time. That's all. Mutual trust and loyalty helped eliminate enemies by drawing them into the fold. The Machine was just one of many successful ventures under his control. At one time, he is said to have owned nearly a hundred properties regionally. With Dawson, city vendors looking to get paid had to head over to the Elks Club and hand over checks made out to the Cohoes Democratic Committee—usually 10% of the amount they were to be paid. Dawson's head honcho and cousin carried the checks from City Hall to the Elks Club. Dawson and his men weren't discreet. Vendors talked about it, but whom could they complain to about it?

Technically, kickbacks are illegal, but a check to the Democratic Committee is okay. It's quid pro quo, but it's a legal loophole. The money went into the coffers of the party, but Dawson would fish some out for himself to buy a car or fix his house or whatever else he liked.

Dawson liked to show off his extravagant tastes, too. Compared to Big Mike's plain, boxy house, which sat close to the road in the lower-class First Ward, Dawson lived in a fancy neighborhood in the Fifth Ward, with a horseshoe driveway and an in-ground pool. He never invited other people over to swim in his pool and let the community pools in town decay until they were virtually unusable.

People were loyal to Mike Smith because he made them feel like they were important, even if he was being expedient. Dawson was the opposite. He acted like a mob boss and made people feel like they were there to serve him. It might be possible that if voters figured this out, they'd stop feeling satisfied. It was not long before I decided to exploit this weakness.

CHAPTER FOUR

GROWING UP WITH "PETE"

We lived on Grant Street, in the Fifth Ward, in a big, five-bedroom Victorian house on the hill, my father bought for back city taxes. The house was so damned big, it took ages to heat up. People think you're rich because you live in a big house. I'd say we were poor as church mice. After my father left us, we had nowhere to go. We had no choice but to stay there.

I mowed the lawn because I didn't want our place to look like a junkyard. I planted flowers around the house and weeded the garden beds. I put the coal in the furnace. If we needed something from the store, I would go get it.

I was only nine years old when my father left. I never saw him much, and I guess I didn't really miss him much either. He was a traveling salesman for Behr Manning. He made good money selling industrial abrasives. He'd come home on a Friday night and leave on a Monday morning. He had affairs with several women, and after he left us, he married a woman from New Jersey.

He would send us about $220 a month. My mother's brother, Walter Wertime, Jr., ran a law practice in town. He could have helped her get a job, but I doubt he ever lifted a finger on her behalf. She was mostly estranged from the men in her family. To make ends meet, Mother kept the thermostat very low, took in renters, and relied on me to maintain the place.

Even though my brother, Tony, was my mother's favorite son, she and I had a good relationship. When I was born, Mother wanted to call me Peter but was afraid everyone would end up calling me

"Pete," a name she didn't like. So, she named me Paul. Everyone ended up calling me Pete anyway.

There was a story about me that my mother loved to tell. When I was four, my parents bought me a pair of roller skates. I put them on, tried to skate down the sidewalk, and immediately fell down. I got back up, keeping one skate in the grass and the other on the sidewalk, skating one foot at a time. Then I switched them over until I got used to skating on each foot. Eventually, I taught myself to skate on both. My mother sat there, watching me all the while. She talked about that for years, like it was a clue to my personality.

I went to work when I was fifteen. My first proper job was at the bowling alley, setting up pins. Before that I mowed lawns, shoveled snow, and delivered newspapers.

Since claustrophobia was one of my mother's many illnesses, she wouldn't go to my high school graduation, because she couldn't stand to be in a crowded auditorium. I sent out graduation notices to both sides of my family, but I didn't hear back from anyone. As I expected, nobody went. I didn't let it bother me. It is not difficult to understand why family really didn't mean much to me. I alone went to collect my diploma, prizes, and awards.

I chose to focus on my friendships and at school. I loved that time of my life. I knew everyone, and everyone knew me. I mixed and mingled with all the different cliques, which helped me get elected class president in my sophomore and senior years. The Catholics would mostly let me hang around with them, and, in turn, I wasn't overly put off by their disdain. A parish priest sent my mother a letter calling my brother and me bastards because my parents had not been married in the Catholic Church. My father was Catholic.

My Uncle Walter was very prominent in town and had a lot of enemies in the Machine, but I never interacted with him much. The first time I met my Uncle Walter, he acted like I wasn't family at all. I was in college and needed to use his law library to write a paper. He was very curt. He turned me over to another lawyer, who showed me how to use the law books.

Uncle Walter was very involved with the Republican Party, both locally and at the state level. As Cohoes Republican Committee Chairman in the 1940s, he was effective. When Thomas E. Dewey was elected Governor of New York in 1942, he made a good showing at the polls in Cohoes. That led to Dewey and Walter, Jr., becoming political allies, an alliance reinforced by their mutual dislike of Mike Smith. When Dewey was running for governor, he promised to break the O'Connell and Smith machines.

After Dewey won, he sent a team of investigators from the State Election Fraud Bureau to question Cohoes City officials, all of them part of Big Mike's machine. It had been Walter, Jr., who dropped the trail of breadcrumbs leading to criminal indictments against Big Mike Smith and his cohorts.

Even if I didn't have much to do with my family, there were still a couple of adults who made an impact on me early in life. The first was my history teacher. She was related to members of the Democratic Machine. I used to challenge her about how they weren't doing much for any of us, and she would say the Republicans wouldn't either, so what was the difference? "It's a reflection of our society," she would say. Years later, I realized she was right, but not because the Democrats were better, but because in our town, we'd never actually adopted the freedoms available to us as Americans.

The other adult who influenced me was my physics teacher, Leo Heslin. He was a good friend and former classmate of the Dean of Admissions at Rensselaer Polytechnic Institute (RPI). One day, Leo asked me where I was going to college. Because I didn't have the money, I hadn't really planned on going to college, although I would have liked to. I had wanted to be a naval officer and dreamed of attending the Academy in Annapolis, but my vision was too poor. Leo asked if I would like to go to RPI, right across the river. Of course, I said yes. He helped me get accepted, but I paid every cent.

One time, I charged my books to my mother. The college accepted that, and I got my books. But when the school contacted my mother, she said she couldn't pay for them. I finally scraped up enough money that term, but by the next one, I had no money at all for books. I had an address for my father, so I tried it; I asked him for the $50 I needed for books. He sent me back a letter. It read, "This is not in my budget."

That was it. After that, I knew I really would have to be tough if I were to have any chance. I knew I had to get that degree. I knew that would be my ticket through life, and it was.

Eventually I learned that I could use the books in the college library when I couldn't afford to buy them. I wasn't allowed to check them out, so I spent hours upon hours there. At least it was warm in the winter.

During the summers, to earn money for school, I tended bar seven days a week at a resort called the Algonquin on Lake George. I enjoyed socializing with the waiters and waitresses, who were also working their way through college.

While in school, I took several technical writing courses. The classes taught me to break things down into the smallest details, which helped when I wanted to learn municipal law. I learned that you have to read the law very carefully and know what the intent is. Like engineering, law is a process. There's a process to designing a bridge. You can't skip any of the steps, or the bridge will fall. I learned the differences between statutory law and rules and regulations, and I found I was good at understanding the law.

It was while I was at RPI that I truly discovered how much we'd been missing in Cohoes, what facilities others had had in their high schools, and how far behind we were from the rest of the country. The most we got from the school board was a basketball hoop that was tied to an oak tree in the backyard of our elementary school. That was about it. They rented space in the Catholic high school for our middle school, so we really didn't have a middle school. The facilities we did have were dilapidated. At our high school, they built a swimming pool, but they didn't have enough money to build a gymnasium, so they converted the swimming pool into a basketball court. You had to walk down into it to play a game. The tennis courts in the back of the school were never maintained. They were always covered with weeds, and the nets were never up.

I had suspected that the resources were there, but they weren't being well managed. Once, while in junior high school, I sat watching the football team practice, and there was Mike Smith sitting in his Rolls Royce watching, too. The grass on the field was two feet high. There were no goal posts on the field, the wooden bleachers were rotting, and the fences were torn. I knew from having seen with my own eyes that the high school's four janitors would sit in the boiler room doing nothing. Those guys would not have had their jobs without Big Mike's patronage, so who knows what Big Mike was thinking, sitting there in his fancy car looking at his handiwork. Why do we have to live like this? That's what I was thinking when I started to learn what kinds of facilities kids from neighboring schools had. I thought, there's something wrong here.

In the spring of 1957, I graduated from RPI with a degree in civil engineering. I had no money, but I had confidence. I also had no attachments to speak of, no favors owed, and no debts. After graduation, I served six months of active duty with the Air Force Reserve and then served as superintendent of construction for a section of Interstate 87. In 1960, I was offered an assistant professorship at Hudson Valley Community College.

It would turn out to be the perfect combination for the ultimate engineering project: dismantling the Machine in Cohoes.

CHAPTER FIVE

A NIGHT NOT TO REMEMBER: 1959

It was April 1959. I had just finished my stint in Texas with the Air Force Reserve. Now, I was back in Cohoes, sitting on a file carton on the second floor of the Remsen Street law office of J. Willard Frament, a defeatist with no organizational or leadership skills. He was also the Cohoes Republican Committee Chairman. He'd been in that position for nearly a decade, during which time, despite the Democrats' abysmal record of service, he'd been unable to unseat them.

Willard had once told me that his greatest wish in life was to be buried in Arlington National Cemetery. I think his World War II experience of commanding a naval destroyer, where a person gets told to do something and does it, had seemed easier to him than politics, where after he'd told his people to do something, he was always having to check that it had been done.

But he'd wanted the chairmanship, so in 1951, the Cohoes Republicans gave it to him. In his first year, he ran for mayor against Democratic incumbent Rudolph Roulier. Willard, who had graduated at the top of his class at Albany Law School, lost by a 20% margin. Roulier, who probably only completed the eighth grade and whose campaign message amounted to "Don't change anything," was now the longest-serving mayor in Cohoes's history.

In 1955, Willard's mayoral candidate choice was Matty Falato, a lovely Italian gentleman from the Fourth Ward and a career gatekeeper for the Delaware and Hudson Railway on lower Main

Street. Matty also lost. Roulier's mayoral rule was approaching twenty years.

In 1959, the window was the widest open it had been in decades for a Cohoes Republican win. Nelson Rockefeller was the newly elected Republican Governor of New York State. Republican Dwight D. Eisenhower was President of the United States. Cohoes Democratic Committee Chairman Warren Smith, nephew of Big Mike, had just resigned, leaving the next election cycle to be overseen by the neophyte, Bill Dawson.

Dawson had made a few speeches that caught even my mother's attention: his drumbeat was that Cohoes was overdue for some serious sprucing up. He wanted to pave and grade the most impassable of streets in town and grate the flooring on the Reavey Bridge. While I was stationed in San Antonio, Mother had sent me a letter that included a newspaper article outlining Dawson's plans. She suggested that this might be a good opportunity for me to come home, apply my civil engineering skills, and exercise my desire for political reform in Cohoes.

My mother was a smart lady, but I could see Dawson was simply savvy enough to acknowledge the obvious. Years of incompetence and low property tax schemes designed to enrich the Democrats at the expense of the city's infrastructure, water distribution, sewer collection, schools, parks, and playgrounds meant the city had reached an embarrassing level of disrepair. Dawson's credentials as a political boss were being tested, and there was too much unrest over the state of decay the Democrats had allowed to spread during their decades in power. Dawson likely knew that could result in a loss at the polls. Directing attention to a few public works projects was just part of the tune-up that he was giving his political machine, which would need to be well oiled and highly functioning in time for the 1959 elections. I would never want to work for that guy.

My mother did have a point about my getting involved in politics, however. I was twenty-four years old. I had a degree in civil engineering and had gained experience working with unions during my time as a superintendent of construction. As a serviceman, I had visited parts of the country far from home and understood that there were better ways of doing things. Other states were expanding and improving infrastructure to accommodate a postwar boom; there were plenty of opportunities for me nationwide, but I still thought of Cohoes as home.

The city's problems had been created and exacerbated by Dawson and his ilk. It would be foolish to hand them the power to fix the city's infrastructure, knowing they would simply maintain the status quo, whereas those improvements were something I had been trained in and loved to do.

So there I was, back from military service, sitting after-hours in a vacant room in Willard's law office, surrounded by cardboard boxes filled with past voter registration books. Willard was instructing me and my lifelong pal, Bill Riley, to go through all the names to see if we knew anyone we could personally ask to vote Republican. Willard didn't have a tracking system per se but was relying on us to come up with our own lists of potential converts.

Willard assigned me to man the polls, to ensure that the Republicans registered during the four days of voter registration—those were the days before permanent voter registration existed in New York State. Over the course of those four days, I observed the Democratic committeemen. They didn't have casual lists of potential personal contacts, unlike Bill and I. They had books filled with the names of every Cohoesier in every ward.

I also observed how each day, in addition to the poll monitors, the Democratic committeemen patrolled from opening to closing time, noting which of their neighbors had not yet appeared to register. They took turns visiting the homes of these missing members of the electorate and "escorted" them to the polls to ensure that they did not miss the opportunity to vote.

I recalled that Vince St. Onge, a friend from high school who'd lived in the First Ward, told me how he'd regularly watched the Democratic committeemen on Election Day walking up and down the line of voters at the St. Patrick's Church polling station, handing out $5 bills to the people still waiting to vote. And so it was that election year: if the committeemen needed to palm out a few favors, that is what they did.

Meanwhile, the Republican committeemen, aside from myself, came, registered, and left.

Willard and his Republicans were also less organized in their approach to promoting the candidates. The Democrats often would brag that they could run a donkey on their ticket and still win. I thought that they had already demonstrated that more than once. Though Willard's strategy to run highly qualified leaders in the hopes they would inspire citizens to think and vote independently, regardless of their party affiliation, was admirable, it lacked the efficacy of the Democrats' unscrupulous method.

Willard had managed to snare Thomas Carter to run for mayor. He was a prize: an Irish Catholic, a registered Democrat, a salesman for General Mills, and a handsome man of medium build, always dressed impeccably in a suit and tie. Carter was from the Fifth Ward, but Willard figured Carter's Irish Catholic credentials would count for something. The rest of the ticket was a mishmash of Independents (former Democrats like Carter who were annoyed with the machine) and Republicans. The Democrats selected Andrew "Dutch" Santspree, the mild-mannered owner of a small stationery store and active member of the local French-Canadian community who'd lobbied Dawson for the chance to run.

Occasionally, Willard scheduled rallies preceded by lines of slow-moving cars, their drivers honking to attract attention. These rallies generally were attended only by the faithful, the hangers-on, and those seeking jobs once the campaign was over.

We had campaign literature that party workers could hand out, but only two of our candidates bothered to use the brochures in a systematic way: French Catholic Ernie Robitaille, Willard's choice for the Fifth Ward aldermen, and Larry Favreau, who was on the ticket for county supervisor.

Ernie was a family man and an accountant with the state. He was personable and a serious campaigner. Gus was my age, an energetic recent graduate of Siena College, a teacher at La Salle Institute, and an officer in the National Guard. Together, they went door to door each night, distributing their brochures and introducing themselves to each registered voter in the wards. Every evening after dinner they would cover a designated area. As they canvassed, I helped them with their mailings and fundraising. Their shoe leather approach, which they reported was being well received, encouraged me. Along with the Sixth Ward alderman candidate, Stanley Kapuscinski, Ernie, and Larry were the only candidates who campaigned regularly door to door.

At rallies, the focus of the Republicans' message was the "intimidation and fear" tactics used by Democrats in power. I believe that anyone in town who paid the slightest bit of attention was aware of the dictatorial tactics the Democrats had been using, ranging from bribery (like the $5 per vote) to kickbacks (like the 10% paid by every city vendor to Dawson and the Democratic committee for every municipal contract awarded). Willard never mentioned these specifics at the rallies, though. He relied on innuendo, his obvious disgust for Dawson, and the Democrats' flagrant disdain for the law.

Dawson's ostentation should have worked in the Republicans' favor. Traditionally, political bosses like Mike Smith and Dan O'Connell kept a low profile, out of the eyes of the opposition and the IRS, even if behind the scenes they called all the shots. Perhaps to his way of thinking, acting glamorous equated with being powerful, and since he was still consolidating his power, Dawson appeared at nearly every public municipal and Democratic Party event. He was there smiling for the cameras with Mayor Roulier during the ribbon-cutting ceremonies for the repaving projects, all of which were timed within weeks of the November election. He was frequently seen driving around the city in his luxurious black Lincoln, another reminder of who held the real power in City Hall.

The Democratic rallies were noisy, well-attended affairs, either because attendance was mandatory or because it was considered a good idea to show face. Dawson appeared at them all, speaking about the new road improvements, highlighting the administration's future projects, and smiling as various other Albany County Democrats assured the crowds of the candidates' impeccable credentials.

On election night, November 3, 1959, down at the Elks Club, the Catholic Keveny Academy Band played to a cheering crowd. In the vacant office above Willard's law firm, the sound we heard was of the window slamming shut on any hope for the Republicans to effectively challenge the Machine that had just swept the polls with the largest plurality ever seen in Cohoes history: Santspree had won with 70% of the vote. Larry and Ernie barely eked out a third of the votes respectively.

Each election result that came in was more devastating than the last: in the First Ward, the Republican candidate got only 14% of the vote; in the Second and Third Wards, the results were barely over 20%; and in the fourth, it was not even a third of the votes. Kapuscinski in the sixth received only 38% of the vote. Willard complained that the voting machines were fixed, but I knew that it was proof the Machine was well oiled, and Dawson had earned his mantle.

CHAPTER SIX

THE INITIAL
CHALLENGE: 1960

The Troy Record reported that during the previous night's celebration of the Democrats' sweep, one of the newly elected aldermen had declared that Dawson's word was now law in Cohoes.

About seven or eight years before this, on a Sunday, I had been home studying for my New York State Regents Physics exam. Two men in suits rang our doorbell. Mother wasn't home, so I answered the door. The men introduced themselves as police detectives. I remember that one of them was Detective Harold Smith. They asked if I would come with them to the station to answer a few questions that would help them out with something. They didn't say what. I think they had been waiting for my mother to leave so that it would be easier to make me come with them. I told them that it would not be a problem and that I would be happy to help.

At the station, they brought me into an empty room and made me wait alone. Eventually, they brought in a kid I sometimes played basketball with, "Duckie" Bessett. About two months before, Duckie, Frank Miazga, Hank Bessett, Jr. (no relation to Duckie), and I had been walking home after a game at St. Agnes's. Duckie pointed to a grocery store on the corner of McElwain and Broadway and said he'd been robbing it regularly through the back window. We all ignored him.

Now Duckie's jaw was swollen, the areas around his eyes were black and blue, and he had stitches across his forehead. He looked directly at me but didn't say anything. I thought, Christ! They beat him! One of the detectives led Duckie back out of the room, while the other detective told me he knew I had been Duckie's accomplice in stealing from the grocery. I told them I knew about it only because Duckie had told me, but that I had never helped him. They repeated their accusations a few more times, but after a while they let me go. I walked home. That was the last of the matter between me and Detective Smith, or so I thought then. Years later, I was sure to close the loop.

My Regents physics exam was two days later. By then, there was a rumor running through town that I was a thief. My reputation had been damaged, I was shaken, and I did poorly on the exam, which still upsets me.

There was a reason why this had been done to me. The Democratic Machine had wanted to embarrass the Republican Party, which was run by my Uncle Walter. He had assisted Governor Dewey in collecting evidence to indict Mike Smith. The fact that he and I never spoke was irrelevant. All people in town knew or cared about was that my mother was a Wertime. The Machine had used intimidation tactics against my family and me, accusing me of something I hadn't done. If there is one thing I hate, it's being accused of something I didn't do. That was 1952. Now in 1960, we had a behind-the-scenes leader of a party who had used the police as mercenary thugs outright declaring to the papers that he was above the law.

I did not want to live in this kind of dictatorial idiotocracy. I contemplated leaving town for lucrative and rewarding employment in other locales, ones with better weather maybe, but I refused to believe that Dawson and the machine, now in 1960, were at the height of their power, and was invincible. I was torn about leaving, but about a month later, still weighing my options, I came across something unusual in *The Troy Record*. It was a public notice that the Cohoes Common Council was to hold a budget hearing after the Board of Estimate and Apportionment submitted its report to the Common Council later that month. Also, according to the city charter, the final budget would be adopted within thirty days, as presented or amended, after the hearing, and an itemized budget would be available for public review at the city clerk's office. This was the first time public notice of a budget hearing had been placed in the paper in the past decade, at least that I knew of.

During the 1959 election, there had been no substantive discussion of the issues, just innuendo and vague promises from the Republicans. From the Democrats we'd had lies and braggadocious claims about the specious public works projects. The budget hearing, however, would be a place where discussion of facts and figures would be the point.

I went to the city clerk's office and hand-copied the itemized budget. I drove to the New York State Department of Audit and Control, which oversees the financial statements of actual expenditures by auditing each city, town, and village in the state every two years. The clerk brought me the 1956 and 1958 Cohoes financial statements and audits. I also copied these by hand.

During the campaign, Willard had made offhand references to the Machine's systematic corruption but had not connected the dots between how the corruption was making fools out of voters and denying them a better quality of life, especially the ones who'd been strong-armed into voting for the Machine.

I wrote a press release. It announced that a committee had been formed to analyze the city's most recent finances and that the findings would be presented at the upcoming budget hearing. The publisher of *The Troy Record*, Frank York, was a Republican. I went to his office in Troy and asked to see him. I introduced myself and told him about the committee. He walked me over to see the paper's daytime editor and said, "Print this." In those days, the editor might shorten or minimally alter a piece, but they often printed articles as they were delivered.

Now I needed a committee. I made a list of all the people I knew who were not sympathetic to the Machine. Harold Reavey: people respected Harold because he wasn't afraid to mix it up. Turk Senecal: Turk didn't have much in the way of skills, but he was usually around and looking for something to do.

I spent days rehearsing what I planned to say, mostly saying it aloud to the wall. I rehearsed questions like, "You've got an allocation in here for redoing the roof on city hall. You didn't do it. Where'd the money go?" I wasn't sure how I would respond when I got the answers, but I was determined to at least get through my questions without my voice cracking.

Mayor Santspree had called the meeting for 8:00 p.m.; I got there at 7:00. The door to City Hall was unlocked. I entered the first floor and walked past the mayor's office; there was a light under the door, and I could hear voices. I went to the council's chambers on the second floor and sat in front. I was the only one there, and I had a rush of fear that this was going to be a failure, with the papers reporting, "Many questions were asked but only a few people showed up."

By 8:00 p.m., Dawson's committeemen were there, as well as what seemed like every city employee. Maybe people had come for the novelty of a public meeting about the budget; maybe they had sensed a spectacle and came for the entertainment. Whatever their reason, I planned to educate them.

Dawson's brother, John, took a seat directly behind me. He was about six feet tall, and just as wide. He had his suit coat unbuttoned so I could see his revolver in its holster, hanging out like a necktie. I was amused that Dawson thought I was so important that he'd thought to bring in an assassin.

A wooden railing separated the council members from the public. Beyond it were the council members' desks, facing the front of the room. Between the two was a raised dais, where Mayor

Santspree sat, facing the public. Sitting to his side was the Deputy Comptroller and Corporation Counsel. Dawson was also on the dais. Big Mike would never have appeared at a public municipal meeting like that; it would have made his influence too obvious.

Santspree announced that he expected it would be a short meeting and that people would be satisfied with what was in the budget. It was his first time presiding over a public meeting as mayor. When it was time for public comment, my knees were unsteady, but I remained composed as I moved to the front of the chambers. I gripped the rail and began.

I asked the mayor and his men to explain why the items in previous years going back to 1957 were costlier now and asked them to justify the increases. Walther Burke, the city's Corporation Counsel, declared me out of order. Only a discussion on the 1959 and the 1960 budget figures were allowed, not any other years, he said.

I continued undeterred. I recited every line item in the 1960 budget, including the salary of every city worker. After I read out the annual salary of a parks department position, the city employee whose job it was shouted that he only made half that amount. Similar signs of consternation erupted as I continued. Dawson and Santspree looked grim.

Next, Harold Reavey compared the costs of neighboring community recreation facilities, all more modern and in far better shape than those in Cohoes. Mayor Santspree declared Harold out of order. He said it was not appropriate to refer to facilities in other municipalities. Harold asked why the mayor would not want to discuss ways to provide the best recreational programs for taxpayer money, such as with the state aid neighboring communities used. More murmuring ensued.

When I got to the question of what had happened to the $30,000 budgeted in 1959 to repair the roof over City Hall, the chambers were quiet. Everyone there could see it had not been repaired.

The mayor said the money had been placed into the general fund. It was the biggest in a series of non-explanation explanations he'd given that night. The hall erupted. Mayor Santspree called for order. When the hall quieted down, I recommended that the budget not be adopted until it had been returned to the respective city department heads to make downward adjustments.

The meeting adjourned around 9:30 p.m. The next morning, the papers reported that Cohoesiers were now on the hook for just over $325,000 more than the previous year to run the city for one year, a tax rate increase of 10%. Santspree cited an inflation-happy federal government as the compelling reason he and the Common Council had approved the third consecutive, annual million-dollar-plus budget without a single change requested by our committee.

I thought the night was a success. We'd focused the public's attention. The notion that voters were being taken for a ride was now part of the local conversation. Letters to the editor in our favor appeared in the paper, including one from a Democrat, John Grego, a chemist, who wrote eloquently in *The Troy Record* about the incompetence of the Machine. I invited him to join us.

Another citizen who'd spoken out against the budget at the meeting had impressed me with his clarity and authority. I had never seen him before, so after the hearing, I introduced myself and asked if he would join our committee. He declined because he was the confidential law clerk to State Supreme Court Justice Staley and so could not get directly involved, but he promised he would help when he could. Frank Landry was his name. Soon he would prove to be a valuable asset to our cause.

I was beginning to get calls from others who wanted to act against the Machine but hadn't known how or hadn't had the guts to do so. People approached me in the street or at the bar sometimes to say thank you. The Citizens Committee, as we came to be called—watchdogs ready to sniff out, dig up, and shake up the corruption—was born.

Still, if Dawson had not mandated that public employees attend, the papers the next day might have read, "Many questions were asked, but only nine people attended." After that night, Dawson forbade city employees from attending budget hearings.

CHAPTER SEVEN

DAVID COMETH FOR GOLIATH

Our growing group began having weekly meetings. We'd drink and socialize, but we were serious about our watch-dogging. I was quoted in *The Troy Record* as having said, "The time is coming when the politician's attitude of 'We shall do as we see fit' will end," yet years later, several reporters would tell me they had simply thought it merely banter between the establishment and the upstarts. The Republicans' abject defeat at the polls had lulled the Machine—and the press—into assuming the Machine's invincibility. They didn't understand that David was coming for Goliath.

Our meetings also served as informal press briefings: reporters were welcome to listen in as we discussed the specifics of the budget and strategized ways to lower costs while improving services. We offered facts and figures, and asked questions of the Machine, including the perennial, "What happened to the money for a new roof on City Hall?" I always had a prepared statement for these meetings, which the reporter from *The Troy Record* would tweak only slightly and then run that week, keeping us in the public eye and keeping up the pressure on the Machine.

We had a good arrangement with the paper. I had learned to deal only with Tommy Thomas, the night editor. He was not a Democrat, and he didn't seem to be in cahoots with Dawson, who was the op-ed cartoonist there. He was a strange duck, though. I'd come in and tell him I had a press release, a statement, whatever. And then he'd say, "Well, go sit over there. I'm busy right now." He'd make me sit there for an hour before he'd talk to me. Every time.

The arrangement lasted until one night, months after the budget hearing, when Tommy said to me, "I can't print any of your stuff anymore." He wouldn't tell me why.

By then, we had a lot of people in our group, so I asked everyone for suggestions for how to get coverage again. Dr. Bill McDonald's wife, Kay, was a real firebrand. She called the paper and told them she was canceling her subscription because they only printed whatever the corrupt administration told them to print.

Brilliant. So, I got a hundred or so other people to do that, and the paper just collapsed. They called me up and said, "Okay, okay. We will print your stuff, but we're gonna lay down the rules for you. Here's what you gotta do. You gotta meet in a public place. You gotta have at least sixteen people there," and they go through a litany of rules for me. "They'll have a reporter there. You'll give them the press release, and he'll report on the meeting, not just the press releases."

That was the work of Alton Sliter, main editor for *The Troy Record*. I know this because years later, after he'd retired, Tommy wrote an article about it, saying that that was what Alton had wanted. Alton had told Tommy, "They're an ineffective group and will not amount to anything."

A historical note: Alton was an honored guest among the so-called celebrities who attended a dinner in honor of Dawson's election as Chairman of the Cohoes Democratic Party in 1959.

I don't know why we had to have sixteen and not twenty people, but I'd round up my sixteen people. We'd have a press release, a meeting to discuss it, and a reporter there to write about it, though he would fall asleep during some of our meetings. That went on for about a year, and then we threw in the towel on the charade. I went directly to Tommy Thomas again, and he got our stuff in the paper.

We held our meetings down at the Roadside Inn. I was always amazed we were allowed in, that Dawson didn't try to shut the place down. The bars in Cohoes got their liquor license from the state, which was Republican, so perhaps the Machine didn't have leverage there.

Dawson's guys sure did attack us, though. The Machine called us amateurs, hippies, obstructionists, out-of-towners, and other defamatory names, which the papers were willing to print. What the Machine didn't do was provide answers to any of our questions, nor did the papers push them to do so. A group of citizens in the lower Fourth Ward especially were riled up over the Democratic administration's failure to communicate.

The group was near the busy, main thoroughfare of South Saratoga Street. Parallel to the street were tracks for the Delaware and Hudson New York City-Montreal lines, and on the other side of the tracks was a quarry and light aggregate plant with kilns which, if the wind was right, produced clouds of dust so thick they blurred the view as they rolled across the vacant wedge of land between the street and tracks. That was the same wedge of land where first the Roulier and now the Santspree administration planned to put a seventy-unit public housing development. Mayors Santspree and Roulier were just the middlemen. They didn't make policy decisions; they executed them as dictated by Dawson. Whether Dawson knew but ignored or was ignorant of the state and municipal laws that were supposed to supersede his own, was irrelevant. I knew them. And if I didn't, I knew where to find them and how to interpret them.

That post-graduation job I'd had working on a portion of I-87, the "Northway," had led to my joining the union and getting my union book. I was promoted from foreman to superintendent when the position opened up. That forced me to quickly learn the concerns of the Teamsters Union, the Operating Engineers Union, the Steelworkers Union, and other unions. I walked away from the job with management and negotiation skills and direct union experience in compliance with relevant federal and state regulations, plans and specifications, and union contracts. I learned the importance of knowing at where to go and whom to talk to.

Part of the city's plans for the housing project was to dump raw sewage from the new units into the often stagnant Champlain Canal. The canal crossed the backs of properties belonging to several residents who feared they were about to get a stinky deal. The housing authorities had ignored residents' several attempts to schedule a meeting about their concerns, so they asked the Citizens Committee to help.

The residents had complained that during the summer months the stench from the canal was already unbearable. Dawson brought out his big guns and had his Commissioner of Public Works state to the press and the residents that there was not any variance in the rate of flow of water through the canal during the summer months. Being an engineer, I knew that the U.S. Department of Interior had a gauge station on the canal to measure the flow of water. I got copies of their reports. They stated that there were no recent records of the flow for the past three summers because the flow had been too low to record. I shared this with the local papers. Then I found the key to capturing Mayor Santspree attention.

I got a copy of the site's engineering design plans showing raw sewage was to be routed from the Housing Authority site, across South Saratoga Street, through residents' yards, and then outfall to the Old Champlain Canal. I checked with the state. There was no permit application on file to develop the sewer line. Even with the permit, the plans would violate state law, which forbade the creation of a new outlet of raw sewage into a receiving body of state waters.

I prepared an engineering report that included a copy of the city's design documents showing the sewer and its outlet into state waters, and an explanation of how this would violate state law. Then I sent the report to the head of the State Health Department, the head of the Water Pollution Control Board, the Federal Housing Administration Commissioner, and *The Troy Record*, which printed it, along with a response from city officials stating that their plans amounted to the cheapest solution without state or federal aid. That was in early April 1960.

There was another snag for Dawson's dirty plan. The Charter for the City of Cohoes is a legal document. It is the city's constitution, the laws by which the city is to be governed by its elected and appointed officials. The Charter calls for public notice on any bonds issued for sewers to state the terminal point of the sewer. Consequently, a map had been prepared showing the properties affected by the "improvement." The Charter also required that the properties abutting the improvement be specially assessed for their portion of the cost based on their front footage. The Charter did not provide for general assessments in which all city property owners pay. City officials had not done this, nor did they plan to do so. The only beneficiary of the proposed sewer was the housing authority, certainly not the residents.

When the state water authorities found out about the sewer plans, they sent Santspree's administration a letter notifying them the proposed sewer line was illegal. Santspree's housing authority director ignored it. Instead, the administration issued a bundled bond to pay for several public works projects, including the illegal sewer.

In early June, I helped the residents on South Saratoga Street file an injunction. The court responded with a summons for Santspree and members of his administration to appear before the

New York State Supreme Court on July 8, 1960, to explain why their plan to sell bonds for the illegal sewer project should not be blocked.

Next, on June 25, there was a morning storm so heavy that it flooded the old polo grounds on Garner Street, on the other side of town from South Saratoga Street. The muddy patch was to be the site of another fifty public housing units to be called Roulier Heights. The storm meant that day's ground-breaking ceremony for the project promised to be soggy. Dawson, various clergy, and a few officials from the housing authority and city hall looked on, smiling as Santspree spoke about helping the city's "dispossessed."

The mud was so deep that Santspree never actually set foot on the site. Rather, he spoke from where he stood on the sidewalk, wielding his shovel. That made it easier for me to walk right up to him and serve him the State Supreme Court summons to show cause why the illegal sewer should be built. The front-page photo in the paper the next day was of Santspree silently reading the summons in the background, with me looking straight at the camera as I walked away.

Santspree's subsequent rants against the Citizens Committee, claiming we were anti-public housing, appeared regularly in the paper; but in the end, the State Supreme Court sided with us. On July 9, *The Troy Record* reported that the mayor and his administration had failed to persuade the court not to issue an injunction blocking the sale of all bonds implicated in the illegal sewer project.

This was doubly bad news for the Machine, since it meant financing for repairs on West Columbia Street was also blocked, since it had been bundled in the $100,000 bond issuance. West Columbia Street, a main east–west corridor, was in deplorable condition. Repaving the street, an important infrastructure improvement that included the entrance to the new hospital slated to open that fall, had been key to Dawson's election promises.

The administration took their loss to the Appellate Court, who sent it back to the Supreme Court, which affirmed its decision. We'd won. City officials offered variations on a theme to the local media: we were troublemakers, out to make a name for ourselves by scaring Cohoesiers into thinking that housing the poor was bad for the city. Santspree called us a small group of disaffected citizens. He admonished us in an interview with *The Troy Record*, saying, "We are all part of this city, and as such we should work together to improve it in the years ahead."

While Santspree scolded, we developed alternate plans for the project, complete with an engineering report. We had the plans printed in the paper so that all of Cohoes could see and judge for themselves. We held public meetings about how our plans would benefit not just people who needed public housing but the entire city. We outlined how obtaining federal grant monies would dramatically cut the cost of clearing blighted areas with existing sewage and other utility lines that could then be used for public housing projects.

There was added incentive to use these suggested sites, as they were all within walking distance of the business district, giving housing project residents easy access to amenities. This would mean lower costs, fewer disruptions to infrastructure, less blight, increased property values throughout, and more business for downtown merchants. It was simple and, more importantly, legal.

We also emphasized how if the administration had followed the city charter as it was legally obligated to do, then special assessments would have to be conducted on people who didn't want the sewer. In other words, the people most negatively affected would be the ones to bear the brunt of the cost. Santspree's response was that the residents' reluctance to pay for the sewer was a good reason to issue a bond so that everyone, not just a few, had to pay for the project.

Since an illegal project shouldn't be assessed at all, and since the injunction had held up funds for repaving our main city thoroughfares, news that the Cohoes Board of Estimates and Apportionment was to hold a hearing on funding the proposed reconstruction of West Columbia and North Mohawk Streets caught my attention. "Any person shall be entitled to be heard for or against said reconstruction of said streets or either of them," the notice read.

The Times Record noted that it was the first time in years that voters had been reminded that the board's meetings were public per the city charter and credited our group for this sudden transparency. The shock of being stung by the State Supreme Court had focused the Machine's attention, the reporter mused.

More than sixty people attended the meeting—not bad for a board meeting no one was accustomed to thinking about. Dawson spoke that night, blaming me personally and everyone else on my side for the work stoppage on the streets. He made sure to add that he and his fellow Democrats would do "all in their power" to work around the injunction and repair the streets.

I fired back that it was Dawson and his people who'd been taxing us for those repairs for years without making them. What had happened to that money? Dawson ignored the question. Santspree called us "disaffected citizens" who wanted to "scuttle" the project altogether.

Corporate Counsel Burke warned that the Council was going to amend the city charter, which would free them up to fund street repairs from other sources. Meanwhile, the new hospital on West Columbia Street was in desperate need of an entrance and of a passable road where drivers could sustain speeds of more than ten miles per hour. City officials closed West Columbia Street and blamed the Citizens Committee for their action. We wondered, what were the other sources?

CHAPTER EIGHT

UNCIVIL SERVICE

Though illegal since the late 1880s, in Albany County patronage was one of the Machine's most reliable tools. I would say it was the life blood of the organization. The New York State Civil Service code stipulates that all municipal jobs are to be awarded to those who have passed a "competitive" exam specifically designed to demonstrate respective candidates' fitness for the available positions. Regardless, that year (1960) in Watervliet, six firemen and four patrolmen were appointed despite answers on their civil service exams having been amended in handwriting other than their own, and in some cases, whole pages of their written exams substituted altogether.

In Albany City, several such irregularities were found in the exams of patrolmen, sergeants, and firemen. In Troy, the local Civil Service Commission did not explain why it refused to fill positions with three persons who'd passed the exam with better marks than those who did get the jobs.

Cohoes was also in keeping with tradition. Before the New Year, William Dushane, a barber who'd served as Secretary to the Civil Service Commission for twenty years under Mayor Roulier, announced that for "business reasons," he was stepping down. More like "business as usual reasons." The new Secretary was William Fuss, an accountant for Berdar's Auto Services. Fuss was also Dawson's brother-in-law and fellow member of the Elks Lodge; he'd once appeared on the society pages with Dawson after a trip to the racetrack.

Fuss's posting in January 1960 happened to coincide with the administration of civil service exams in Cohoes. There were seven positions held by provisional appointees. Including these seven provisional workers, there were nearly fifty test-takers in all, a Cohoes record. As an experiment, Harold Reavey and I also sat for the exam.

In February, the state announced that only twenty-seven of the fifty test-takers had received high enough scores to qualify for municipal civil service. With a qualifying score of 82 out of 100, I was among those who'd passed. Harold also passed. None of the provisional hires had qualified in the exam.

A month later, only two of the seven spots had been filled by top qualifying candidates; yet, two of the disqualified candidates had been allowed to remain in the exact jobs they'd had before despite failing to demonstrate competency in their roles. Fuss had authorized reclassification of one of the positions from clerk to typist and another from clerk to confidential investigator. New titles, same duties: no need to follow the law.

Neither Harold nor I wanted a civil service job, but we had what we did want: evidence. Harold wrote to the state's Civil Service Commission President explaining the situation and requesting an audit in Cohoes. Kaplan responded that there would be one that summer.

In October, the state auditors released their findings. It appeared that at least one police sergeant, a lieutenant, and a fire captain were employed under circumstances "too striking to be a coincidence." Plenty of others who'd qualified for the slots had not bothered to apply for them. Why? City officials had "discouraged" them from applying, the auditors found. The auditors reminded Fuss in their report that such discouragement was not in the "competitive spirit." It was also illegal, they added.

The audit unearthed more sins. Job reclassification was all too common, as were the number of demonstrably unqualified candidates throughout the ranks. Sometimes a job was left unfilled entirely if it could not be reclassified. Then, there was the fact that salaries were too low to attract truly qualified candidates in the first place, according to Kaplan. It was a classic Albany Machinery move: why pay one person $5,000 annually when you can pay two people $2,500 a piece, and get twice as many votes, including the two workers' families?

Kaplan concluded that the overall effect was "a prevailing attitude of apathy in Cohoes toward the merit system.

CHAPTER NINE

A GAME OF CHESS, MR. CHAIRMAN: 1961

After a winter without West Columbia Street, the City Council did in fact vote unanimously in 1961 to amend the city's charter. It was a chess game. Dawson wanted to clear us off the board so he could move ahead with his inadequate road improvements and illegal sewer. The administration's proposed amendment not only allowed for general assessments for public works projects but also gave Common Council discretionary authority to conduct special assessments in the name of public improvement. This was a very deliberate addition.

We asked for a public referendum on their amendment, but Santspree ignored us. He endorsed the amendment, saying there was no good reason not to. The word to the press was that now the city could reissue bonds and move ahead with the necessary repairs to West Columbia Street. Their amendment to the city charter made it easier to bypass the residents whose property would be disturbed by the sewer line. The unamended law would have required that they pay special assessment taxes to cover a public works project that abutted their property. But they didn't want the project, and wouldn't benefit from it anyway, since their sewer lines were already in operation. If the administration had proceeded by the book, there would have been push-back. They got it from our group anyway.

The only way to stop their amended law was for us to act in accordance with the state's Home Rule Law. We would need to muster enough petition signatures to force the issue onto the ballot during the next general election in November, something that no one had ever tried to do in the history of Cohoes.

Whimsical tax assessments were classic features of the Machine. They had figured prominently in Big Mike's play book. Dawson followed suit. That year, Harold Reavey, several property owners on South Saratoga Street, and my mother had all seen their property taxes suddenly raised concurrent with our appearances at city hall for budget hearings. It was blatant retribution for going up against the Machine. We agreed to keep that fact to ourselves, in case people got spooked, but we did file certiorari proceedings (legal process by which a property owner can challenge their tax assessment) with the State Supreme Court and won reversals for each of them.

The administration's emphasis on general assessments seemed to be about fairness, but in fact, it fueled the Machine's legal arms against us by adding the power of discretionary assessments. In other words, they could do whatever they wanted. When Machine operatives wanted to punish or reward citizens by way of adjusting property assessments up or down, there would now be the discretionary assessment, which could be anywhere between 0% and 100%.

Now, when financing projects they didn't want to call attention to (such as an illegal sewer line that was core to plans for locating a public housing project on a site that was demonstrably among the worst in town for poorer residents to live and at a cost to people who would be unable to use the sewer line despite paying for it) there was the general assessment: spread the pain, individuals will feel the impact less, and no one will complain loudly enough for us to have to listen.

We filed not one but two petitions. According to New York State City Home Rule Law, to successfully force a referendum on their amended law, we would need to file a petition with the city clerk, signed by 10% of the voters who voted in the last gubernatorial election. The Common Council could either accept or reject our petition. If rejected, another petition with an additional 5% of the voters from in the last gubernatorial election would be necessary. Then we could force the amendment to be on the ballot in the next election without the need for Common Council approval.

We would need to follow the same formula by petition to put our own law on the ballot. Based on the 1958 voting rolls, I calculated that we would need 1,065 signatures for each petition's first submission and half that amount for the second petition. My plan was to turn the Machine's own tactics against them. We would organize and go door to door to get the necessary signatures. At our weekly meeting at the Roadside Inn, I told Norm Bowen from *The Times Record* our plan. We would file two petitions, one against their amendment and another in favor of adding ours to the ballot in the general rather than a special election, since that would have a greater turnout.

Our law would abolish the Council's discretionary assess ment powers. Norm reported on our open invitation to Mayor Santspree and the aldermen to initiate the reversal of the law by signing the petition themselves. We goaded them to vote according to their own consciences, rather than voting as they were told to by the powers that be. We never got a call.

Fifteen members of our group volunteered to petition citizens. The best chance we had for getting the number of signatures we needed would be to skip the First, Second, and Third Wards and stick to canvassing the Fourth, Fifth, and Sixth. We rehearsed what the canvassers would say and how to answer any questions. At the end of two weeks, we had 1,533 signatures against their local law and 1,494 in favor of ours. They were presented to the Common Council, and as predicted, they rejected them. We went back with our second round of signatures: 494 and 688, respectively.

In September, Santspree announced that he and his Council would not challenge our second round of signatures, despite many "irregularities" in our petitions, because "It would be more in line with the policy of this administration to allow the petition to stand and to place the matter before the voters of this city and to allow them to decide which of the two local laws is desirable." A lovely gesture from the front man for the real man—Dawson—who had not allowed the referendum in the first place. Clearly, he anticipated that we were on a crash course toward embarrassment.

While the chess game of local laws was in play, the Council took advantage of their power to use general assessments for public works. They issued bonds for $220,000 to pave West Columbia Street and an additional $100,000 for other poorly maintained roads that were aggravating the electorate who were annoyed by their busted tires. Tempers had been flaring over the state of the roads, so the administration declared paving West Columbia Street a public emergency, pre-empting competitive bidding.

My uncle George Wertime was awarded the contract. He had contracts with General Electric, Ford Motor, and the Saratoga Racetrack. He was a highly reputable contractor, but he didn't like Dawson. In fact, not long after, he and Dawson got into a fight. As a Republican, George refused to support the Democrats with 10% of his contract. Instead, he told Dawson he would need to add 10% to the contract. He wasn't going to let Dawson ever put him at a disadvantage. The fact that he got the job anyway tells you how badly Dawson wanted those roads paved.

In late July, the eastern section of the street was repaired and reopened to traffic, but the western portion was still in disrepair. As a result, drivers had to take a circuitous route to leave the city. In August, the hospital board wondered according to the press when the road would open so they could finish the entrance to their new hospital. This might have meant that public opinion leaned in our favor, but I thought our chances were grim. It was our first election challenge against the Machine's well-tested, long-undefeated boots-on-the ground organization.

The one thing I did think was in our favor was that we were asking voters to do something complicated. I doubted that Dawson was concerned about whether his constituents understood what they were voting for or against. Our voters would have to be more sophisticated than Dawson's. Mass "voting practice" clinics would be our key strategy, along with out-organizing the masters of organizing. We had less than two months.

We started with writing thank you letters to the 2,118 voters who'd signed our petitions. Then we sent follow-up letters outlining the differences in the local laws and the importance of voting against theirs and for ours.

We then identified which residents citywide were most likely to support our position from a fiscal perspective. We determined there were about 2,500 homeowners currently registered; explaining the difference in the local laws and how each would affect them was key to our strategy. We made a list of registered Republicans and Independents not already on the homeowners or petition signature lists. We combined everyone into a master list, according to ward and district, and asked them to register to vote in the November election.

Next was ballot class. For us to succeed, we would need voters to reject the first law, and then take an extra step to vote yes for our law. We made a copy of the ballot that showed first where to find the administration's law and how to vote no against it, and then, where to find our law and how to vote yes for it. We mailed this practice voting ballot to every person on our master list. We also ran ads in *The Times Record*, announcing times and places where we would demonstrate in person how to read the ballot. We also offered a volunteer-run phone bank that people could call if they had any questions.

We trained our thirty poll watchers in the election laws and on their legal authority to mitigate voting violations. We would not be intimidated, and could be aggressive if necessary to ensure fair voting access. The Machine had well over a hundred poll watchers. On Election Day, the Machine employed its old playbook, with the committeemen and party workers marching people out to vote for their chosen county supervisors. We did not have enough poll watchers to cover all twenty-four voting districts; so we focused on the First, Second, and Fourth Wards, all Democratic strongholds where we knew violations were most likely to occur.

The polls were open from 6:00 a.m. to 9:00 p.m. The day felt long, but was mostly uneventful. About a hundred of us gathered at the Roadside Inn that night, waiting for the results.

Unbelievably, the people of Cohoes defeated the administration's amendment (discretionary special assessments) and supported ours (general assessments only). Our amendment had won every Ward but one and taken 64% of the vote citywide. In the First Ward, we had won by 1.6 to 1 and in the Fourth, Fifth, and Sixth Wards, by more than 2 to 1. Our strategy had worked!

Check mate.

CHAPTER TEN

APATHY BECOMES ACTION: 1962

The following year, 1962, was relatively quiet for our group. We held dinner dances, clam steams, and other social events to grow our membership, raise money, and create a sense of mission. We continued to educate our members on issues by having our monthly meetings at the Roadside Inn. Reporters were always invited to attend. Analyzing the city's finances and determining if what had been promised was being carried out was always a focus of ours; we were always gathering data for use during the annual budget hearings, which were now popular spectacles in town.

The Santspree–Dawson administration still was not receptive to change and said as much. The discussions of the 1962 annual budget, as per usual, did not include the previous year's financials because they were unavailable. However, we demonstrated with our usual facts and figures how the city could reduce the tax rate and still increase services. Santspree called us obstructionists, derided our "lack of experience" compared to the administration, and adjourned the hearing without adopting the budget. He passed it quietly, out of public view, a few days later. Santspree told a reporter that he'd considered our questions, suggestions, and objections, but concluded that they "did not carry sufficient weight to merit changes."

At that same budget hearing, Santspree and Corporate Counsel Burke warned the capacity crowd that if the mayor didn't like what a person had to say or how it was said, that person would be ejected from the chambers. If things got heated, he'd stop the meeting in its tracks. And, incidentally, there were some new rules: no one was allowed to speak more than once, and the mayor could interrupt people if he thought they'd spoken too long. Carl Engstrom, one of our group's leaders, objected to the rules, since the previous rules had not been officially rescinded. The mayor ignored him, and the crowd erupted.

If the mayor and his men had sought to manage a mutiny with their rules, they couldn't have found a better or funnier way to set one in motion for the next meeting. About a week before the hearing, the mayor had a partition constructed straight across the City Hall council chamber, with the ironic explanation that the city needed more Civil Defense classrooms. We wrote letters to the mayor and the paper listing several alternative classroom sites. What's done is done, came the reply, and anyway, the partition had only resulted in the loss of twenty seats. We started calling it the Berlin Wall.

A week before the hearing, we circulated a petition. In it, we said if the administration couldn't relocate the classrooms, then they should relocate the hearing so that all who wanted to attend could. We offered several viable suggestions in town that would accommodate a large crowd, such as a school auditorium. By the day of the hearing, we had 350 signatures, but nothing changed. The morning after the meeting, *The Troy Record* ran a photo of Cohoesiers mobbing the entrance of City Hall to get a seat. The photo covered a third of the page above the fold and was captioned, "Like at a Caruso Concert!" referring to a popular singer at the time. "They came in numbers, and they came early to Cohoes City Hall last night...standing room only would be the rule," read the rest.

In the fall of that year, we invited the mayor to tour the city's recreational facilities with us to see firsthand their condition. The invitation included a parks and recreation status report and photos we'd taken that demonstrated how run-down our facilities had become.

Meanwhile, we had been waging an information campaign, revealing that the city was eligible for state aid earmarked for parks and recreation program improvements. Even if the city did apply for the aid, we reported, the facilities were run down; the state was dubious about what might happen to the aid if granted. Public funds had a way of disappearing in Cohoes. The previous year, twenty playgrounds had been budgeted, but only ten had opened. A pool in town that was budgeted to remain open for twelve weeks had only been open for ten. We asked the administration to consider forming a Parks and Recreation Commission. This went nowhere, so we threatened to take it directly to the citizens by way of another referendum. Still no response.

Our last-chance-before-the-winter-snows tour of the parks was set for an early November day at 10:00 a.m., beginning with Sunset Park. The mayor was another no-show.

The Troy Record ran an article based on our parks and recreation status report. They had their own photos. One showed crumbling cook-out fireplaces at Lansing Park. It was captioned, "Fireplace or Rubble?" Another photo, taken in July, depicted three young kids sitting on the side of the wading pool in Sunset Park. The pool was filled with dirt and a rusted, abandoned car.

That week, the administration announced that over the winter there would be an enlarged basketball program, a new golf instruction program, and beginner ice skating lessons. Such were the fruits of a meeting between the mayor and none other than Matthew J. Grestini, Jr., the city's new Commissioner of Parks and Recreation. The programs never happened. Quelle surprise!

CHAPTER ELEVEN

DECLARATION OF WAR: 1963

After three years of being called to account for mishandling funds, losing in the state Supreme Court, losing the assessment law ballot, having its patronage exposed, and mismanaging facilities, the administration still had not fundamentally changed. We still didn't know what had happened to the money raised to replace the roof on City Hall. We still had blight, lousy park facilities, overcrowded and deteriorating schools, and poor roads. Nothing was being done about the detritus of a formerly dazzling mill town. Cohoes was no longer a place for families to build their futures.

That year's (1963) budget hearing was evidence of the Machine's intractability and its deranged refusal to acknowledge that times were changing. By then, the popularity of the meetings had piqued the interest of local television news crews. Santspree refused them entrance, insisting that their flashing lights were distracting.

The hearing had lasted several hours and played to a full house. As was now customary, despite city taxpayers being told they were on the hook for increase in their tax bill, there were no previous years' expenditures for review. The mayor maintained that they weren't needed. The budget was the "envy" of neighboring towns, he said. We could not verify the amounts of several judgments against the city (judgments the Citizens Committee had brought light to; the administration would not acknowledge them). Sewer litigation costs, contractor costs, and the precise calculus for the tax hike were all similar mysteries.

Technically, the budget was illegal anyway, since it did not include the cost and revenue for the water department as required by the city charter. We also questioned funding requested by the Urban Renewal Agency. The city engineer said he needed the money to develop new electric and plumbing codes. This was suspicious, since development of codes is the job of a Planning Commission, not the Renewal Agency, and the state had developed standard codes for adoption.

Santspree claimed that the city would be applying for the state's Water Pollution Control grant. Too late, I informed him. The grants were fully funded but limited, and while neighboring towns had made the cut, the funds now were depleted.

And so it went. The obstruction. The incompetence. The arrogance. We could continue to expose them, but exposure was ineffective against shamelessness. If the administration would not change its tactics, we would have to change ours. To run for office in a citywide election and win would be a Herculean task, but I could see no other solution.

The following month, at our third annual winter banquet, I addressed our members, now more than 300 strong. As watchdogs, we'd failed to shift the administration's indifference, to inspire them to reverse the deterioration of city facilities, or to provoke the Common Council into striking a stance of any kind. The Machine of old had at least looked out for its own. Now it served only a few. It was run by reactionaries and fueled by petty threats, but it was still well oiled, even if we had exposed its incompetence and beaten its members at the polls during the referendum. What we had in our favor was that the Machine was getting old. It lacked any young blood.

So, we announced our intentions to form a party and run against Dawson's Machine. This was met by our membership with cheers.

Dawson also cheered the news when he heard about our plans. "It's the best news I've heard tonight. They haven't got a chance," he apparently told his fellow diners at a bird-watchers' club banquet that same night. He did hedge his bets, though. "We don't recognize them," he added.

Gloomy old Willard Frament, Cohoes's Republican Committee Chairman, was quoted in the papers saying there was no future for a third party in Cohoes.

CHAPTER TWELVE

ROCKY PLAYS POLITICS

Because of what the citizens had shown was possible, people who used to be intimidated by the Machine were now speaking out and enjoying their strength in numbers.

The School Improvement Group had sprung up as part of the new activist spirit in town. It was led by a fiery woman named Millie Freije who, on behalf of her group, had filed suit against the school board for not holding board meetings in public, which was the law.

Most of the public schools in town had been built just after the American Civil War. The high school was so overcrowded that it had to run one group of students in the morning and another in the afternoon. The Machine had controlled public school board appointments for more than forty years, and it had allowed the board to operate in secret, never formally hearing the concerns of parents.

Around the time we'd announced we were running for election in the spring of 1963, the school group hired Paul Coughlin, a local attorney, to petition the State Education Commissioner to mandate the school boards to have their meetings open to the public. That was where I first met Paul. The Commissioner ruled in favor of the school group.

It was a positive but small step. Both the Citizens Committee and the School Improvement Group decided that the only course to get rid of patronage in the public school system was to have an elected rather than an appointed board. To do so would require state legislation or the Machine's Common Council approval. We would need a state assemblyman and senator to introduce our bill for an elected school board. The problem we had was that in our case, both were O'Connell Machine puppets. We knew they would delay, delay, and delay.

The assemblyman in the district just north of Cohoes was a Republican, Dick Bartlett. During my summers as a student at Rensselaer Polytechnic Institute (RPI), I tended bar at the Algonquin Hotel on Lake George. During the day, I delivered ice to the campers on the islands. I got to know Dick because he and his family would camp on one of the islands every summer. We developed a pretty good relationship.

I called Dick and asked for a meeting. I told him we needed his help introducing a bill that would allow cities to petition for referendums to have elected school boards instead of appointed ones. He replied, "Yeah. I'll be happy to do it, Paul. But you need to go to your local guy first, even though he's an O'Connell guy. Then, if he won't do it, I'll do it."

Always the pecking order with the Machine, but that's what we did. We had a narrow window to submit the bill. I wrote a letter to the O'Connell guys, Assemblyman Lifset and State Senator Erway, requesting that they submit our bill for a referendum. I told them we only had ten days to submit it and asked if they could please respond within seven days. Meanwhile, Frank Landry drew up the wording for the bill. As written, the bill would enable cities with a population of less than 125,000 to hold a referendum on an elected school board question if at least 10% of voters signed a petition requesting such a referendum take place.

Lifset and Erway responded not to us, but to the press. They were quoted saying that they had "never heard of a civic organization setting [about] in such a manner." Senator Erway stated that he would have to consult with the Mayor of Cohoes, the Cohoes School Board, and other mayors across the state for fear that giving over the school boards to elected officials might result in Communist infiltration and could demoralize teachers. We had a lone registered Communist in Cohoes, whose name I forget, and one Socialist—my mother—who was agoraphobic, so I doubt she planned to subvert the local schools.

Dick Bartlett it was. He introduced our bill in the State Assembly. It passed 117-25 with strong bipartisan support. In the State Senate, the bill passed 32-28. Our bill got statewide support and was endorsed by the State Congress of Parents-Teachers Association and the State Teachers Association. All we needed now was the signature of Governor Rockefeller, something we were confident we would get.

Two months later, Rockefeller vetoed the bill. People across the state were stunned. He complained that the bill had not designated the term of office, nor stipulated control over the occurrence of the referendum.

I personally wrote Rockefeller a letter informing him that his objections were not legally valid. I quoted him the very language we'd used for the provision of term of office, as well as why we couldn't legally stipulate control over the frequency of referendums because that would have run up against state and federal constitutions.

It didn't matter. We were victims of Rockefeller's vanity project. He wanted to have a mega-mall built in Albany as a monument to himself, but he knew he couldn't get the necessary bond approved in a statewide referendum. So he made a deal with Albany's Mayor Corning, which is to say he made a deal with O'Connell. Rockefeller would veto our bill so that the Machine could keep control of the Albany City school board. In exchange, Mayor Corning would use the county government's powers of eminent domain to acquire the land Rockefeller wanted to build the governor's tribute to himself. Otherwise it would require a statewide referendum for the state to acquire, which Rocky knew would not pass. That's exactly what happened, and the county leased it to the state for hundred years.

The only way we were going to get an elected school board was to have the Common Council enact legislation for a referendum for it. With the Democrats on the council, that would be a colossal task!

CHAPTER THIRTEEN

THE KEYS TO A SUCCESSFUL CAMPAIGN

Willard had taught me the power of a good organization because he didn't have one. You've got to have good candidates and you've got to have money, but you've also got to have an organization. My theory was that if I had no money but quality candidates and an organization, I could still win. If I had lousy candidates and no money but solid organization, I could still win. It's the organization. That's what it's all about.

We had a lot to organize. From our announcement in February to the election in November, we had eight months to recruit candidates, raise money, and build and assign our troops. There were twenty-three voting districts that would require recruiting and training approximately 180 poll watchers and committeemen to ensure a fair election and to see that our targeted voters registered and showed up on Election Day. We already had about thirty trained poll watchers who had participated in the 1961 Local Law election. We had 300 members, no money, and no candidates for the fifteen open offices. Our membership was concentrated in the Fifth and Fourth wards; we had little if any in the other wards.

The Machine, on the other hand, had well over 200 trained election inspectors, committeemen, and poll watchers, and it controlled the police department, which assigned an officer to every polling place. They had incumbent candidates, about 6,000 registered party members, and plenty of money in their coffers. Dawson worked at one of the local papers and, even though no one knew it at the time, secretly owned the City of Cohoes's only newspaper, *Newsweekly*.

Recruitment is like a less dubious version of a pyramid scheme: once we recruited our core members, they recruited their neighbors and friends. Dr. Jay McDonald recruited patients who were loyal to him and wanted to help. Once, Dr. Jay referred a patient to me who he said wanted to help. I knew the guy was a Dawson mole, so I gave him a petition for circulation; I told him to get twenty signatures and return it to me, and then I would give him another petition. I never saw him again. Dawson was always trying to infiltrate our group.

Once we had our recruits, we had to educate them. We produced a fact booklet describing in detail our platform on education, the city budget, street maintenance, water, urban renewal, sewers, snow removal, and recreation. We distributed it to our members and workers so they were well versed in the issues and messaging.

This enabled them to educate the public about why they should vote for our party. That's something the press can't and won't do. As watchdogs, we had regularly recorded budget hearings and other meetings. We transcribed the recordings and mailed them out with comments to voters we thought would be most aroused by the content. This was extremely effective in providing details the papers often didn't report. I told my team, "We've got to have our own newspaper." We called them fliers. We used a drawing of a Minute Man to symbolize our always being alert and protecting the voters. Our motto was: "The only liberties the people have are those they exercise."

We had to share our plans with the public. The directions had to be very specific: this is our plan for recreation; this is our plan for water pollution control; this is our plan for running our civil service commission; and so forth. Most politicians avoid specificity, lest they be caught out. They're committed to being as unspecific as possible, so they don't ever have to genuinely commit to anything. I'm the opposite. I think if you want to get the people to come with you, they've got to know unambiguously what you're going to do. They feel more comfortable, and you have greater credibility.

We also had to get the word out and keep up the drumbeat. We developed a distribution system in each voting district and fine-tuned it so that our weekly fliers could be distributed to every home in the city in four hours or less. When we got closer to the election, we started delivering our fliers twice a week. Today social media would be a similar tool.

To win an election, you need good organizational leaders and good ground organization. Your team has to know the issues. They must be willing to canvass door to door. You have to man the polls. You have to make sure your people know the election laws so they can see that they are enforced so it's a fair election.

Once we had our candidates, I appointed a campaign manager and coordinator for each ward who coordinated with the city-wide campaign. Our campaign workers spent all of September and October going door to door, handing out campaign materials in person or leaving them materials under the door mat—it's a federal offense to open anyone's mailbox if you're not the mailman, so we didn't do that. We also put up billboards all over town in key locations.

Another thing we did was identify who votes in which elections. There are people who vote in presidential and gubernatorial elections, but won't vote in local elections. We knew if they were Machine voters, they would have voted in the local election. We could identify them because back then, the county kept public registration books on who registered to vote in each election—federal, state, and local—so we could make a special effort to recruit those voters. We sent out 2,000 letters saying something like, "Hey, we know you vote for president. We know you vote for governor. You don't vote for local elections, but this local election is very important. Here's our platform, and here's why it is important."

We focused on educating these voters and getting them to the polls. We'd call them to remind them to register. There were always four days for voter registration in October. Then we'd call them up again to remind them to get down to the polls. The objective of this program was to increase voter turnout by 1,500 votes that would be favorable to our cause.

We told *The Troy Record* we would not bother to run if we did not believe we could out-perform the Machine. The paper reported that we were organizing at a voting district level to petition for candidates and that we promised that our candidates would be qualified and beyond reproach.

Part of our canvassing efforts entailed gathering enough petition signatures to nominate our people as third-party candidates. It was nearly the same procedure we'd used before to get the local law on the ballot. That made for seven petitions in all: one per ward for the aldermen slots and one citywide petition for the mayoral and two assessor spots. It was a full-scale operation using the lists we'd created in 1961 when campaigning for our local law. Our campaign managers and coordinators made sure their teams knocked on every door and spoke with every person at least once.

Sometimes, things got lost in translation. Bill Riley was petitioning on South Saratoga Street at the house of a family whose English wasn't fluent. Bill explained several times that it was a "citizen's petition." The man who'd answered the door suddenly shouted into the house at his wife, "Olga, come down here and sign this, and you will become a citizen."

We could not file the petitions until we had enough signatures nominating the mayor, two assessors, and an alderman and supervisor for each ward. We were up against the clock, since by law, we only had about three weeks, beginning in mid-August. By the time we got all the candidates lined up in the Second Ward, we only had one week to collect enough signatures before the deadline, but we made the cut. After we'd filed the petitions to get our candidates on the ballot, Dr. Jay, the Citizens' mayoral candidate, sent a signed letter to each person to personally thank them, tell them why he was running for mayor, and explaining our platform.

That was another lesson I learned from Willard. The Republicans never thanked anybody. I always made sure we thanked voters. I always felt that once you got people involved, whatever their contribution was, they needed to be recognized and acknowledged for it. Otherwise, it's a missed opportunity to consolidate support. Thanking people makes them feel like they are a part of something, which in this case, happened to be our revolution to overthrow a corrupt machine.

My campaign philosophy was, "We're going to win by one vote. So, you'd better keep working. You'd better keep going. You'd better get as many people as you can. You are going to win by just one vote."

We held a series of rallies in the different wards to introduce the candidates to voters. This meant more door-to-door knocking. We had to personally invite people to the rallies. It was an opportunity to hand more fliers out and talk about the subjects that people in that ward cared about. They usually wanted to hear the solutions we were offering. The finale was the citywide rally. It was a grand affair. People love a parade. We got bands and floats and all that good stuff. You have to create excitement.

Once you get them fired up, be sure you get them to the polls. You have to identify who your voters are. How do you do that? With us, we identified that the Republicans were all potential voters for us, because they're supposed to be against the Democratic machine. The Independents were all potential voters because they weren't aligned with any political party. Lastly, we could rely on a certain number of independent Democrats because they were not Machine Democrats.

To raise money, we sold "McDonald" neck ties and shirts with the minuteman mascot on it. Our auxiliary women held bake sales in the central business district on Remsen Street. Ralph Robinson, our candidate for county supervisor in the Fifth Ward, recruited people to fundraise and canvass. He did it in a highly professional, organized manner, giving each recruit a certain number of businesses or citizens to contact in order to raise funds, much like sales targets. He gave them all pledge cards and brochures that explained the benefits of our party.

Good fundraising. Good candidates. But most importantly, good organization.

CHAPTER FOURTEEN

THE HUNT FOR CANDIDATES

Dr. Jay McDonald was a kind, soft-spoken man. That did not mean he was easy to work with. You'd be in conversation with him about one thing, and he would suddenly jump up and start talking about something else. A lot of people thought he was scatterbrained. He was considered one of the best diagnosticians in the capital region, in any case.

I think the way he was had to do with something he'd seen in World War II. He came home from the front lines well-decorated, having served as an army captain and surgeon. He used to tell me stories of how he'd been behind the German line in Italy, near Rome. He'd been part of the amphibious landing at Anzio. The landing stalled, and they were shelled for several days by the Germans who had the higher ground. Eventually, the Allies pushed the Germans back and were able to advance. He would often talk about seeing dead soldiers, Allied and German alike, holding photos of their loved ones. Dr. Jay would say they haunted him, all these men who died alone, far from their homes.

There were six or seven doctors who'd been elected mayor of Cohoes, which stands to reason because they have a broad reach across socioeconomic divides. Jay was a second generation medical professional, as was Jay's brother, Dr. Bill. They both made house calls. Between the two of them, they probably took care of more than a third of all Cohoesiers. Jay cared for anyone who needed it—old or indigent; he was good to everyone.

His one vice was betting on horses, and he was pretty good at it. He didn't want his wife, Virginia, to know. One time he insisted we go to New York City. He told Virginia that we needed to go for a meeting with the regional office of the Department of Housing and Urban Development. He had me make the appointment. I couldn't see any reason for the meeting. But he insisted, said it was necessary.

We got in the car and drove the three hours to New York City. We went in. We had a ten o'clock appointment with regional director at Housing and Urban Development. It was ten o'clock and his aide came over and said that he was going to be a bit late. Eleven o'clock rolled by and we were still waiting.

Jay said "Come on, we're leaving."

I said, "Leaving? Jay, don't miss our appointment. You came all the way here to New York to see this guy. You can wait a little more—" He was gone before I could finish my sentence. I got in the car and he said, "We got to make the daily double at Aqueduct." So, we got over to the race track at Aqueduct and he played the daily double.

He said, "Don't ever tell Virginia!"

I said, "Don't worry, I won't." I never did.

I'm not a gambler, so I said, "Look, Jay. I'm going to the bar and I'll watch the races there. When you're done, come get me."

He found me at the bar and counted his winnings. He said he had enough to buy a boat. I don't know how he got that past Virginia.

He didn't make much money as a doctor, maybe $35,000 a year. He and his family lived comfortably, but he wasn't extravagant. He charged the people who could afford it but didn't charge the people who couldn't. He knew my mother didn't have any extra money lying around and that her brothers and my father weren't good for it either, so he took care of me at no charge. Usually, I just needed stitching up after football injuries.

Jay liked the company of most people, wealthy or poor. He was a very good golfer, and he loved to hunt and fish with anyone keen to go with him, including me. It was a big deal for me to be seen as good enough company for an educated person like Jay. He wasn't a father figure so much as a big brother. Jay and I would go skiing, too.

I wanted Dr. Jay on the Citizens Committee ticket. Others had suggested I run for mayor, but mayoral duties like social affairs, ceremonies, and board meetings didn't interest me. We needed someone extroverted and affable, someone willing to shake hands and rub elbows. I'd rather be the guy that gets things done behind the scenes. Jay was an icon. People loved him. They were certain to vote for him.

After the Citizens won the 1961 referendum, Jay told me that if our group ever decided to form an independent party, he'd want to run for mayor. This was before Jay and Virginia's only son, Jimmy, was killed in a skiing accident. Jimmy was only twenty-four years old. He left behind his wife and a little daughter.

Jay, like many aggrieved parents, fell into a depression. He quit his practice and became reclusive. Sitting there with him one day, he told me he no longer wanted to run for mayor, although he said he'd consider tax assessor or alderman.

I'm losing him, I thought. The pressure was on me to get Dr. Jay on the ticket. I had to do something.

It wasn't until June that things fell into place. Jay still had not committed. I wanted Harry Marra on the ticket, too. Harry was my dentist. He would always talk to me while he was taking care of my teeth, so I knew he was anti-administration. Dr. Harry was hanging back, though, waiting to be sure Dr. Jay was on the ticket. But time was running out to secure other candidates, canvass, and file petitions with the Board of Elections to get on the ballot.

I went to see Harry. "Harry, Jay said he would run for assessor if you run for assessor," I lied.

"Let me go talk to Sally. Call me back this afternoon and I will let you know," Harry said. About an hour later, I called him back. "I'll run," he said.

I ran up to Jay's house. "Jay, I was just talking to Harry Marra. He told me he'd run for assessor if you'd run for assessor."

"He did?"

"Yes."

"Well, okay then, I'll run."

That was a Sunday afternoon. I got Jay's picture and a brief biography. Then I went to Harry's and got his. By Sunday night, I had delivered it to *The Troy Record* so the announcement could be made before either Jay or Harry could change their minds.

With Jay and Harry on the ticket, our recruitment really took off. Bob Curran, who'd been a World War II naval officer, agreed to run for alderman in the Fifth Ward with Ralph Robinson running for the ward's county supervisor. Frank Rourke, a nuclear scientist whose seemingly unlimited energy meant he would be at full throttle even after days without any sleep, was running for Fourth Ward alderman. I had wanted Harold Reavey in that slot, but the Citizens Committee voted on Frank instead. I think they feared that Reavey, who had a habit of getting into a bar fight every now and then, would be too blunt about things.

Jay recruited Earl Radcliffe, a labor union leader, to run as alderman in the Third Ward and Irene Rivet, a pillar of St. Joseph's Church in the local French-Canadian community, for Third Ward county supervisor. Dr. Jay also got John Krawiec to run for county supervisor in the First Ward.

We recruited army veteran Frank Colaruotolo, who ran a grocery store in the Sixth Ward, to run for alderman there. There was Alex Rymanowski, a personnel supervisor, for alderman in the

Second Ward, and Howard Curtin, a salesman, for alderman in the First Ward. Paul Bourgeois, who had a master's degree in education, was running for county supervisor in the Fourth Ward. Bill Diack, superintendent of the RPI field house, ran for supervisor in the Second.

Our ticket was complete except for Mayor. Again, time was running out for petitioning. We needed Dr. Jay to commit to running for mayor that night, so I called up Harold. He was the perfect guy for the job I had in mind. I knew that Dr. Jay and Virginia were dining out that night. I told Harold to put on his best suit and tie and go get Jay out of the Century House restaurant right away, for an emergency meeting with all the candidates at Dr. Harry's house. Soon, Harold had Dr. Jay and Virginia in tow.

After some discussion, Virginia convinced Dr. Jay to run for mayor. I took the slot alongside Dr. Harry for the two tax assessors, and now we had our complete slate. Most of us had college degrees and were already seen as community leaders in our respective wards. We were a mix of enrolled Republicans, Democrats, and Independents. We had a doctor, a dentist, two engineers, a small businessman, a steam fitter, a machinist, a teacher, and several retirees. We were predominately Catholic, representing all the major ethnic groups in town: Irish, French, Polish, and Italian. Plus, our ticket directly represented labor's voice. Our candidate for the Third Ward, a notorious Machine stronghold, was Earl Radcliff, President of Local 393 of the International Brotherhood of Pulp and Paper Mill Workers, AFL-CIO. Plus, nine of our fifteen candidates were registered Democrats.

A lot of our candidates also were decorated World War II veterans. Having veterans gave us a twofold advantage: it stirred patriotic sentiment among voters and helped raise the question of why Cohoesiers would tolerate anything less than democracy. These war veterans had put themselves in harm's way to help restore freedom to our allies; when they came back, they saw things differently. They could see the effect of the local oppression. They wanted to fight for freedom at home in Cohoes. They talked about that when they campaigned, and people listened.

We were required to have 1,000 nominating signatures on the petitions, but we filed twice that many signatures with the County Board of Elections, in case there were any challenges to signatures. We had received 4,000 signatures, but we held half back in case the O'Connell-controlled board said they accidentally "lost" them. If that happened, we would just file the rest. I kept a copy of all the signed petitions just in case. I was surprised when I asked someone at the Board of Elections to sign a receipt saying he had received all of them, and he signed it. I think he was just as surprised to be asked.

We'd had some great help writing our petitions from a guy by the name of Frank Landry. Frank was the confidential clerk to State Supreme Court Justice Stanley. Frank was somewhat small in stature, but had a commanding presence and spoke with steady authority. We used to call him the Bantam Rooster. Because he was a lawyer, he knew how to write petitions so they wouldn't be challenged or thrown out, since the language could be quite technical. Because of his job, he had to help us in secret. No one besides me knew of his involvement.

We got a picture of Dr. Jay in *The Troy Record* looking over all the signatures. The newspaper printed the number of signatures for each of our candidates and the number required. This was a good bit of psychological warfare: Hey, we're coming for you, and look how many people support us!

So that was us. We were now a third party. We had our candidates, and we were ready to run. When news of our ticket landed in the paper, Dawson gave a speech at The Elks Club, which doubled as the Cohoes Democratic Headquarters. He talked for about fifteen minutes, about twelve of which were dedicated to listing what he disliked about us. He said our third-party ticket was just the Republican Party reconstituted, only dirtier, meaner, and willing to lie. He pledged that his party's ticket—his same old has-beens running against our roster of college-educated professionals, war veterans and heroes, union laborers, and community leaders—would run a clean campaign and that they would win based on their record of achievement and dedicated service.

The paper ran our collective responses:

"I find it comical when the administration tries to create the impression that they know how you vote yet are not aware that I have voted for the past four years," said Dr. Jay.

"It was ironic that the Democratic chairman pledged himself to a clean campaign and then devoted 90% of his text to smearing the Citizens Committee," said Bob Curran, our candidate for Fifth Ward alderman. "A Democrat is one who supports the principles of the national Democratic Party, and a Dawsoncrat is one who supports the principals of Chairman Dawson," said Frank Colaruotolo, our Sixth Ward candidate. Howard Curtin asked, "What happened to the $30,000 appropriation for a new City Hall roof?"

The stage was set.

CHAPTER FIFTEEN

GO FOR THE JUGULAR

Nobody in the press, not even my pal Tommy Thomas at *The Troy Record*, thought we were going to win. Just before Election Day, I asked him to predict. He said, "You might win an alderman."

I knew that if we were going to make an impact, we'd have to elect the mayor and the Common Council—full sweep. Otherwise, we were not going to bring about any change at all. If you're going to run, you're running for the whole show. You can't run halfheartedly. I mean, if we didn't get elected, we were done. Goodbye. That would be it.

The press followed the thinking of the Machine operatives, whose reaction to us from the beginning was, "You are amateurs. This is for the professionals. You are not supposed to do this. Republicans and Democrats. That's it. It's our turf. The Democrats are in, the Republicans are out. Democrats are out. Republicans are in, but no outsiders." That was the attitude. There was an operational ignorance that helped keep this structure in place, so I knew making them play defense would work. We were going to hit them hard.

A key to our strategy was that we'd flood the town with our fliers characterizing the Machine for its corruption and neglect of our city and using facts and photos. We had plenty of issues to choose from, including corruption, education, recreation, streets, union endorsement, and *Machine Politics*. Mayor Santspree, meanwhile, said there were only two issues: that we were extremists, obstructionists, anarchists, liars, and political terrorists, and that he had a solid track record as mayor.

They had a picture in the paper showing Dawson and Santspree standing with a real donkey, the Democratic Party symbol, between them. We used the photo in one of our fliers, with the caption, "Which one is the jackass?"

We'd pull them off their game. They'd have to respond, and while they were doing that, we would tell voters all the great things we were going to do for the city. We would show a picture, and we'd be very specific: "We're going to build a multi-purpose community center. This is what the building would look like—here's a model we had drawn up of the building. We're going to fill in the canals and put green spaces on them. Here is a model of what the playgrounds would look like, and so on." For us, specificity meant accountability, and that was a good thing.

Today, the election season begins at the start of the year and seems to last forever. Back then, things were different: we kicked off the campaign in September for the run-up to the elections in November. The Democrats held a clam steam and claimed that 2,000 people attended, but I doubt the turnout was even half of that. Walter Burke, Santspree's corporation counsel, was their master of ceremonies. He was reported as saying that they had two opponents in this election: The "Get Even Party" and the "What Have You Done for Me Lately Party." I guess we were the latter of the two.

Dawson and Santspree also talked about their "achievements," including paving eighty streets. That was something, since just a few months before, they were saying they'd paved forty. They talked about how they'd painted all the fire hydrants, which was true, but what they hadn't done was fix the ones that didn't work. Which do you think would be more important to voters?

They also talked about how they'd established an ambulance service in town. They left out that the reason they'd had to do that was because they'd gone so long without paying the private service that we'd shared with other communities that the owner of the company shut us off. Plus, he wouldn't pay his "tribute" to Dawson.

In October, we examined these "achievements" in a flier. First, we looked at Dawson's street improvement program. We showed one street they had paved where the concrete was scaling and flaking apart. It was so bad that it had to be repaved with asphalt. We headlined this as the cover up that it was. We also had a picture of me measuring the thickness of concrete on a different street Dawson's people had just paved. It showed me pointing to the ruler, illustrating that the street was under the contracted specification of eight inches. The simple math on that amounted to a difference of more than $4,000 for that street alone. Where did the additional money go? We put it this way in our flier: "Whose pocket did that neat little bundle wind up in? Could it be one of those rolls flashed across the gaming tables in the Elks Club?"

They tried to come back at us, saying all the good things they were going to do, except that everybody in town knew they weren't going to do these things because they never had.

Santspree had publicly stated that the city had parks and playgrounds in all six wards. We rebutted that in our next flier, stating that there were no parks or playgrounds in the Second or Third Wards. We showed a rendering of a park and playground that we'd create by filling in the power canal in the Second Ward using federal money that was available for just such projects. We also showed a model we'd had made of a proposed community center that would serve the youth in these wards.

Dawson responded by publicizing a rendering of their planned urban renewal program using federal money, with a northeast sports center that would begin construction immediately. I pointed out in the papers that this wasn't possible to do, since federal certification would take two years. We were doing everything we could to keep them on their toes.

We pivoted and ran a flier with an aerial photo of Dawson's house. It showed his horseshoe-shaped driveway in front and in-ground swimming pool in back. Alongside that, we ran the photo of two kids sitting on the edge of the public wading pool in Sunset Park with an abandoned car in it and another one of two kids playing on a makeshift raft in one of the abandoned, polluted power canals. The caption read, "This is where your children play, and this is where Dawson plays." They would be hard images for Dawson's people to defend.

Every flier was another chink in their armor. We distributed one explaining that we could win the election with hard work. We wanted voters to know they were not wasting their vote if they voted for us. Using previous voter registration records, I determined that there were approximately 880 Republicans, 7,000 Democrats, 2,000 Independents, and 1,500 potential voters who typically did not vote in local elections. I then forecast that the Citizens would get 480 Republicans, 2,500 Democrats, 1,800 Independents, and 1,500 of the potential voters for a total of 6,280 for the Citizens, 4,700 for the Democrats and 400 for the Republicans. We had strong data to support our claim that we had a chance to win.

We also explained that the Machine might threaten to know who voters cast their ballot for, but unless they were in the booth when ballots were cast, Dawson's people had no way of knowing who voted for whom. Voter privacy was protected.

Every time one of our fliers went out, Dawson's gang would countered with fliers of their own. Every time we'd hold ward rallies, Dawson's people would schedule one right after. *The Troy Record* reported that Dawson was having trouble catching up with us.

Democrats typically get the endorsement of the unions, and therefore their opponents come across as anti-union. We had to break that perception. Getting union endorsements was another way we hit Dawson hard.

First, we ran a union member, Earl Radliff, President of a local union. Dawson started bragging that the Troy Area Labor Council, AFL-CIO, endorsed the Democratic slate in Cohoes. That was not true. We countered in a flier and a press release in *The Troy Record* that Ed Duval, representative of the Amalgamated Clothing Workers Union, AFL-CIO, had stated his union "has not and will not" endorse the Cohoes Democrats. Then other members of that council came out and said the same.

Joseph Petretti, representative of the International Brotherhood of Pulp, Sulphite, and Paper Mill Workers, AFL-CIO, wrote an open letter to the voters of Cohoes, published in the Record, specifically supporting our Third Ward candidate, Earl Radliff. To *The Troy Record*, Dr. Jay presented a petition signed by hundred members of the United Steel Workers of America who protested the use of their union name to endorse the Democratic ticket in Cohoes. The coverage in the paper was headlined, "Union Support Split."

We hit at Dawson's gang in other ways, too. We turned one of their most trusted weapons against them: we got people to register to vote. It was a large undertaking. Registration days were the Friday and Saturday of the first and second weeks of October from 10:00 a.m. to 10:00 p.m. for all twenty-three voting districts. We had to train and assign people to man all of the polling stations in advance.

We used the Fifth Ward as our model for training people in the election laws and in manning the polls. We got out the vote by going door to door. We used our system of identifying voters who had been willing to sign our petitions, the ones who had voted in presidential and gubernatorial but not local elections, those who were Independents, Republicans, and "friendly" Democrats. The first day of registration produced 1,110 more registrants than the year before. Some districts in the Fifth Ward tripled the number of registered voters over the previous registration period. Meanwhile, during the first weekend of voter registration, Santspree sent the Assistant Chief of Police, Assistant Chief Kielb, to one of our lower wards and ordered our workers to cover up any windows that had our campaign advertisements in them, citing local election laws that prohibited electioneering within hundred feet of a polling place. The problem was that law only pertained to Election Day, not registration days. We took down the covers over the ads.

They tried again. We caught some city workers tacking up Santspree posters over our Vote Jay posters. The police stood by as a half dozen of our campaign workers tore down the Santspree signs. Then the cops arrested our folks and hauled them off to the city jail. Kielb started booming about not tolerating any further deliberate mockery of Cohoes law enforcement. I showed him pictures I'd taken of city workers placing Santspree posters over Jay's. Our workers were free by evening. That night, I wrote a letter to Mayor Santspree, telling him to publicly instruct all city employees, including the police, to stop breaking the law and to remove all the "Vote Santspree" signs from city equipment. I walked it over to *The Troy Record* and that pretty much took care of that.

In the four days of registration in October, we helped to get 11,000 voters on the rolls, a record for any Cohoes local election. With a rapid growth of enthusiasm, organizational efficiency, and record enrollment, I started to believe the tide was turning.

CHAPTER SIXTEEN

RALLY AND EXPOSE

The following are some notes from my strategy book for the 1963 election:

- Organize enough workers to man the polls for four days of voter registration.
- Create our own newspaper and deliver our message with our own distribution system to every doorstep.
- Create additional special mailings targeted to specific groups.
- Have ward rallies to introduce the local candidates for alderman and county supervisor.
- Have a citywide rally and a parade.
- Organize tough, scrappy guys and girls to man the polls on Election Day.

These guidelines helped me stay focused through the battle for the election that fall.

Every time we'd outsmart the opposition, I'd feel pretty good about it. There's no question about that, but the run-up to the election was getting heated. The odds were against us, but we were ready.

Our success was met with retaliation and hostility. In mid-September, someone threw glass bottles filled with printer's ink at our billboards. *The Troy Record* ran a photo of it, which turned out to be great publicity for us, since it was likely Dawson's people had done it. Ralph Moore, one of our supporters, was a builder from the Fifth Ward. He'd had a falling-out with Dawson. He woke up one morning, went outside, and saw that his red brick house has been splattered with white paint. It was a mess. The local papers ran Ralph's offer of a $1,000 reward for the arrest and conviction of the culprits. That was a lot of money back then; however, it turned out that Moore threw the paint on his house to make it look like Dawson's people did it.

We'd electrified the town. The press certainly was interested. In September, *The Troy Record* ran a week-long series of articles reminding Cohoesiers of their political history. The first article reviewed the rise and fall of the Republican Party in Cohoes. It featured Dr. Jay's father, who was the last Republican mayor in town; the Democrats had been in power from 1921 to 1963. The City Election in1959 was the year to forget, when Republicans had their worst local defeat ever. The second article featured Dr. Harry Marra as "Give 'em Hell, Harry." It noted his frank, outspoken manner, "When aroused he possesses the tact and diplomacy of a wounded water buffalo." The third article recapped the Mike Smith dynasty, the succession of his nephew, Warren, and most recently by his grandnephew, Bill Dawson. The fourth article featured me and chronicled my leadership of citizens into a third party. The fifth was about how the Democrats credited their unprecedented twenty-eight consecutive years in office to their many accomplishments, including eighty recently paved streets. Dawson was quoted as saying that on Election Day our party would get "a real trimming." The sixth focused on the Republicans. Until I read it, I hadn't known that "The Republican Party has been on guard at the polls during these past years, and it has been a thankless job. The citizens of Cohoes owe a deep debt of gratitude to the Republican inspectors," so it was good Willard had told the reporter. The final article focused on our candidates. I threw in the dig, "The voters of Cohoes want honest government but have never been afforded the opportunity."

The articles nicely teed up our run of rallies. We had one in each ward every week. They were an opportunity for the voters to meet their alderman and county supervisor candidates and vice versa. The rallies also gave the press a chance to cover the micro-local issues in each ward and for us to give rebuttal statements to the "Dawsoncrats" claims.

The biggest event was our citywide rally held eight days before the election. We teased it with our fliers saying things like, "Don't miss this rally! There will be a big revelation! It's a big exposé on the Machine!" We sure riled people's curiosity. The surprise was that I had affidavits from builders and various city vendors who had been coerced into contributing cash to Dawson's guys in order to get or keep city contracts.

We held a citywide motorcade followed by a parade as a lead-up to the rally. As part of the parade, there was a float from each ward, marching bands (including a Spirit of 1776 fife and drum corps), and all the candidates in convertibles. The press reported that a crowd of more than 1,000 people watched the parade. Dawson's people had a parade, too, on the night before Election Day. He boasted they had more than 2,000 people in attendance, but the paper reported there had been only several hundred.

The rally took place at the Cohoes Theater. The candidates waited in the theater manager's office as the crowd took their seats. Frank Rourke suddenly burst into the room, running around with his hands in the air, and screaming we had to do something because the Fire Chief had closed the front door and would not let anyone else in because the theater was at capacity. Then he ran out as fast as he'd come in. The rest of us just stared at each other, speechless.

The crowd was over capacity, so they had to close the door to block further entry. I had foreseen this happening, so I had already arranged to have a sound system set up outside the theater for the rest of the crowd. The next day, the paper reported that after 1,300 people filled the theater, the police were hard-pressed to control the hundreds left outside waiting to get in.

I began by telling the crowd that I had signed affidavits from developers and city vendors proving corruption by the Machine. One was from a builder who'd had to make a $100 "contribution" to Dawson and the Democratic Committee before he could get a building permit that only cost $27. I told the crowd about another city vendor who'd had to pay a $500 "contribution" before he could get his permit. The icing on the cake was when I revealed that the swimming pool built on Dawson's property was built in part with city resources, as stated in the signed contractor affidavits. The crowd was stunned into silence.

Dr. Marra spoke about our dim prospects for economic development with Dawson and Santspree in charge. He said no firm would settle in a city plagued by a corrupt government and school system. Bob Curran presented a slide show with aerial photos on how we might attract more industry. Dr. Jay announced that yet another union, the International Typography Union, denied they were endorsing the Democratic ticket in Cohoes, even if Dawson said otherwise.

Then we showed a film narrated by Dr. Jay listing all the ways Dawson was a tinhorn politician, followed by our plans to improve our community. It was our own version of an FDR-like "fireside chat." We were showcasing what Cohoes could and should be. It was quite effective.

The film played on local television as well. We bought the time for it to run as a public service announcement and advertised the airtime in our fliers. When the time came, guess what happened? Instead of our film, it was Santspree and his own announcement. It turned out the station was in O'Connell's pocket. I would have said we'd been had, except their little film was so awful, they did us a favor. The response from viewers was along the lines of, "Jesus, who would vote for those clowns?" When we asked the people at the TV station what happened, they maintained that it was an innocent mix-up.

On the Saturday evening before Election Day, we were having a rally at the Marconi Club in the Sixth Ward. The City Marshal strolled in and served Dr. Jay, Dr. Harry, and me with a summons: Dawson was suing us for libel and slander. Dr. Harry read the summons. It did not state an actual complaint we were to answer. It also didn't specify any amount of damages, which Dr. Harry noted, "There is no amount of damages listed because Dawson couldn't figure out what his reputation was worth."

The next day, Dawson made a statement to the press: "I held my temper through the campaign...but found I could not hold it any longer."

I urged Dawson to pursue the suit. It would enable us to subpoena his personal records, as well as city records, launching the biggest investigation in this area in years. "I wish Dawson all the luck in the world!" I announced to the group. Everybody laughed because it was hilarious. We never heard another word about it from Dawson.

The summons was signed by Dawson's attorney, Seymour Fox, so we did a little digging and found a county record of a deed in his name. I asked Frank Landry to do a title search. He found that Fox had purchased a piece of land in the administration's urban renewal zone just before it was designated as such, meaning he'd purchased it at a rate far below market value. On the day before the election, *The Troy Record* ran a story chronicling Dawson's suit and our subsequent discovery of Fox's land holdings. In the article, Santspree called us liars and said Fox made the purchase because he had faith in the city of Cohoes. We ran our own version of Dawson's attempt to intimidate us and headlined it, "DAWSON'S LAST GASP."

Time to vote!

CHAPTER SEVENTEEN

ELECTION DAY AND A NIGHT NEVER TO BE FORGOTTEN

Tuesday, November 5, 1963: Election Day. Often, at least in upstate New York, the second Tuesday of November is long, wet, and dreary. Weeks before, Frank Landry had recruited twenty-one special state attorneys general to man the polls and help us enforce election laws. That was still in the era of phone booths, so we armed our poll watchers with lots of coins to call for assistance if there were any problems. We set our headquarters up in the back of the Marra's Drug Store with a bank of twelve phones.

We were ready. Our poll watchers, committeemen, and their runners knew their tasks. All that was left for me was to ensure the integrity of the voting machines.

A few days before election day, all the voting machines, by law, were available for inspection at City Hall. The machines were not computerized but had cylinders that responded to levers that in turn corresponded to a single candidate. An official group, including a Democratic and a Republican custodian, would examine the backs of the machines at the same time, and everyone had to agree that the tally counters all read zero. Of course, when we looked to see if they were all at zero, they weren't. They already had three or four votes here and there. Dawson stood silently scowling at us as the machines were recalibrated. After they all were reset to zero, we closed the backs of the machines and sealed them. The seals were not to be broken until 6:00 on the morning of the election.

Ray Contois, custodian for the Democrats, offered me a ride on Election Day. I considered this an important role to ensure that the machines delivered an honest election. They had a police car for the day to quickly fix any voting machines that might malfunction. It would be Ray, the Republican custodian, and me. We were on call for any problems in any of the districts. I had designated a campaign chairman for each of the wards. They were responsible for seeing that their people were there at 5:30 a.m.

Election Day is long. The polls don't close until 9:00 p.m., so you've got to have a plan to relieve your volunteers. Ray and I also monitored election-related calls on the police radio as an added safety measure.

Then we got a call that in the Sixth Ward; a voting machine had gotten stuck. When we arrived at the polling station, Bill Riley, the Campaign Manager for Frank Colaruotolo, was pacing outside. He was beside himself. Bill was so agitated, the poll watchers made him step outside. Apparently, Frank's mom had entered a voting booth and somehow jammed up the machine. It was the only machine at that station, so no one else could vote until it was fixed. Because of the delay, people standing in line were getting tired and walking away. Ray and I had a look, and it seemed hopeless to us unless we removed the back of the machine and release the lever; however, it was against the law to do so. Protocol dictated that the seal be put on, the machine be sent to City Hall, and have a new, sealed machine sent over. That would have taken over an hour, easily, but where would that leave the people still waiting in line?

Ray asked me, "What do you want to do?"

I said, "Ray, take the back off. Fix the problem."

So he did. We could read the dials on the back of the machine, and Jay was ahead—not by a huge amount but enough to notice. We fixed the stuck cylinder. As Ray and I were leaving, Bill asked me what he should tell Frank about his mother's vote. I said, "Tell Frank we don't need it."

The Troy Record reported that there were resident challenges by our poll watchers in several districts. Kielb, the same Assistant Police Chief who'd held our guys in jail, was quoted saying that in twenty-three years on the job, he'd never seen so many challenges about residency or other voting violations made on Election Day.

Still, for the most part, it was a quiet but long day. Jay went around to all the polls that day, per my instruction. I had arranged to meet Jay at his house after the polls closed. I found him sitting there in his recreation room, smoking a cigar, drinking a Crown Royal and ginger ale, watching television as though nothing much was going on. I had instructed our campaign manager in the Third Ward, Santspree's home district, to call us with the voting results as soon as he had them. The phone rang. Dr. Jay had beat Santspree in his home district, 178 to 143, and citywide 5,917 to 4,455. Virginia wasn't home; she was a poll watcher in the Third Ward, one of our toughest and most likely to be corrupt, doing a recount. Santspree wouldn't accept the loss easily.

"Congratulations," I said to Dr. Jay. "You're the new mayor of Cohoes. You gotta get down to St. Michael's pavilion."

Ever humble, "Okay," was all he said.

I had runners from each district bringing in the results to St. Michael's where we had a tote board mounted on the stage. The results were there for all to see. When I got there, it was so crowded I could not get to the stage. We had won the mayor, assessors, three aldermen and three county supervisors. It was a landslide victory. Our candidates in the Fourth, Fifth, and Sixth Wards had creamed the other guys. We lost the Second Ward by seventeen votes and the Third by twenty-five. The Republicans barely had made a dent: forty-one total votes in the Second and fifty-two in the Third.

The local Catholic Keveny High School band was waiting at the Elks Club for Dawson's victory parade. He had to send them home. Soon after the polls closed, Santspree decreed a state of emergency. He told reporters, "We may have to use tear gas." The Associated Press included that in their story that ran nationwide.

The next day, the Albany *Times Union* headline read "CITIZENS WIN IN COHOES." All the Capitol District papers ran editorials admitting that they never thought we would win. They described our meteoric rise from organizing as a political party into a force that had decimated the two major political parties in town.

Tommy Thomas's paper, *The Troy Record*, told it best, "For the Albany County Democratic organization, the Cohoes setback brought the first crack in many years in a wall long believed indestructible...the extent of the Citizens Party victory in Cohoes surprised practically everyone."

The best article of all ran in the *New York Herald Tribune* Sunday edition. Describing our journey from the beginning, the headline read, "Amateurs CAN Lick City Hall-Here's Proof" and stated that what we did "offered an inelegant lesson to amateur political reformers every-where: If you want to oust an entrenched power, aim for the jugular."

The morning after the election, after a late breakfast, I went to collect on the only bet I had made during the election. In early September, I had received a phone call from my Uncle George. He asked me to come to his office; he wanted to talk. When I arrived, he told me that the Citizens would need the Republican Party endorsement to win and that my Uncle Walter wanted to meet with me. I told George that the Republican Party endorsement was the kiss of death. He said, "You do not know what you are up against. The Machine will throw everything against you." I bet him a bottle of Canadian whiskey that we would win, and he took the bet. He asked me to meet with Walter anyway, and I agreed. I went to

Walter's office. It was the first conversation I had with him since that one brief interaction we'd had when I was in college.

Walter said that we would need the Republican block of 2,500 votes. I disagreed. I told him the Republicans would get only 400 votes. Walter looked at me as though I was some kind of hippie and gave me a slip of paper with a phone number, "If you change your mind, give me a call," he said, and that was that.

Turns out I had underestimated Willard's vote: he got 404.

George gave me two bottles of Canadian Club: one for our bet, the other for, as he said, "Beating the bastard." George told me how Dawson had wanted a 10% kickback for contracts, but he'd refused.

My next stop was to see Tommy Thomas, night editor at *The Troy Record.*

"How much money do you think winning this election cost us?" I asked.

He said, "The rumors I hear are that Rockefeller gave you $50,000. That's the way these rumors go."

I replied, "Well, he didn't give us $50,000. It cost us $9,000. That's what it cost us."

"Where did you get the money?"

I told him, "Ralph Robinson's fundraising. Selling neckties. The minuteman shirts, the bake sales, all that. That was it. We didn't have a patron. We did it ourselves."

We the people did it ourselves.

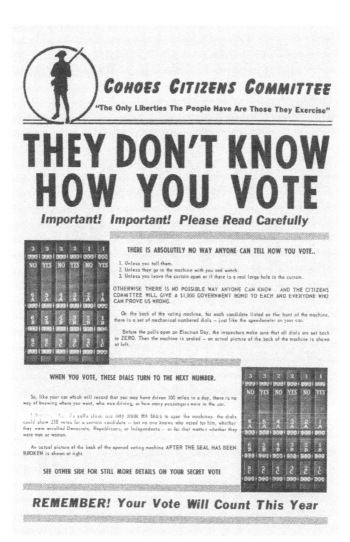

We introduced our four page flier in the 1963 Election as a key tool to get our message across. We organized a distribution program in which the flier would be delivered to every home and business. (program) This front page of this flier was part of a campaign to convince voters that the Machine did not know how you vote. The Machine had created the fallacy over the years and we needed to debunk it if we were going to win the election.

In the 1963 Election the Democrats eventually adopted our messaging tool.
From left to right: Mayor Andrew Santspree, the Donkey and William Dawson,
chairman of the Cohoes Democratic Party; their flier provided us with some
political humor.

One of the issues in the 1963 Election was the endorsement of labor. Dr. Jay got a union leader to run for alderman and his union publically supported him. Other unions followed suit and publically announced that they were not supporting the Democratic ticket in Cohoes. Dawson had publically announced that they supported his ticket. We had broken the long string of union endorsements for the Democratic ticket.

Election night: the great upset and the beginning of the reform movement (November 5, 1963). Dr. Jay at the Citizen's Election headquarters and the tote board showing his overwhelming victory along with the newspaper head-line in which his father won the Mayoral race in 1921. Courtesy of the *Albany Times Union*

PART TWO:
REFORM

CHAPTER EIGHTEEN

THE OBSERVER

When I was ten or twelve years old, my mother sent me to a YMCA summer camp. Most of the boys there were bigger than I was, as usual. There, we had a canoe tilting contest. We'd paddle out into a circle, stand up, and use poles with boxing gloves on the ends of them to clobber the guys in the other canoes. The goal was to knock everyone else into the water. The last guy standing won.

So, I was up there in the front of the canoe. The guy behind me in the canoe, Al Sterling, was from downstate in Nyack. Al was older than me. He and the rest of these guys were huge. I said to Al, "Let's go and get it over with." He said, "No. We're not going in yet. We're staying behind. Keep still and let them go in and fight it out. After that, we're going in."

I listened to Al. All the rest of the guys were in there duking it out. Finally, Al said it was time. So, we went in, and I was up against this gorilla of a kid. He was enormous. I wound that pole up like a baseball bat. I didn't want to hit him. I wanted to hit the canoe. I hit the canoe, tipped it over, and won, and Al said, "I told you!"

The moral of the story was don't go in too fast. See how a thing plays out, then determine a strategy. There are times to go rushing in, but only if it's to put out some kind of fire. This lesson remained in my mind during the events that unfolded after the election.

All the Citizens candidates, ward leaders, and district committeemen had essentially pledged to be reformers. They threw in their hats to support our party platform—policies, projects, and programs—spelled out during the campaign. Because of that, we beat the Machine, the power players.

However, after the election, some elected candidates thought it was their charisma and smarts that got them elected, rather than the team and the principles they ran on. They became power players, the very thing we had run against. They had agendas of their own and began to coalesce with other power players.

History tells us that after a revolution either the good guys (reformers) purge the bad guys (power players), or the bad guys purge the good guys.

The first meeting we had after the election was at Harry Marra's house. All of our elected officials were there. Turk Senecal was there as the Fifth Ward Campaign Manager, and Jim Bottum as the treasurer. Harold Reavey, Dr. Jay, and I attended, but none of the other members of the executive committee (unsuccessful candidates, ward campaign managers, and party officials) had been invited.

I objected, saying that the new committee should include all the candidates who ran, even the ones who lost, as well as the campaign managers. They had been just as integral to the election. If we hadn't had good candidates in the tough wards to draw votes away from the Machine, we could have lost the election altogether.

Harry Marra insisted, "We won. They lost."

This was a terrible sign. "All the campaign managers should be here, too," I said.

It was a panic for power. They did not want more people involved because it would dilute their power to select department heads.

"Bill Riley, our Sixth Ward Campaign Manager, isn't here because he's hunting," I said.

Harry said, "If he's not here, then he's not part of it."

There were two appointees I could not get behind. The first was John Brady for City Court Judge. Everybody was against him. Brady was a troublemaker. They say it takes a carpenter to build a barn, and it takes a jackass to knock it down. Brady would knock down barns one after another. There always had to be conflict and drama any time Brady was involved.

But Dr. Jay had the power to appoint whomever he wanted, and in this case, that meant John Brady.

The other person I didn't think was the right man for the job was Turk Senecal for Public Works Commissioner. He could give directions, but he didn't take them well. He was in the National Guard. Whenever he came home from duty, suddenly his huge freezer would be filled up, because he was stealing steaks and butter from the Guard. He didn't try to hide the fact; he told people unabashedly, including me.

Turk was ignorant in a lot of ways, and he was shifty. His value to our campaign team had been that he didn't have a job. We had him run errands and do odd jobs. For example, when we needed someone to go down to the State Comptroller's office and copy all the financial statements by hand because the state people wouldn't copy them for us, we got Turk to do it.

Looking back, I see that Rourke had been lobbying Harry Marra to support Turk for Public Works Commissioner, while Turk had convinced Bob Curran and Ralph Robinson to support him for the role when he was their ward Campaign Manager. Rourke wanted Turk because he thought that he could control him. Turk probably thought that he could control Rourke, too.

Turk should not have been put into a position of governance. Giving him that kind of power was just an act of patronage. That's why Harold, Jim Bottum, and I were against him. Bill Riley, a good friend and supporter of mine, would not have voted for Turk. Everyone knew that, which was likely why he hadn't been invited to the meeting.

I did not want Turk in that office, but Rourke became irate. Ultimately, he got his way, and Turk was named Commissioner of Public Works, the largest department.

After the three of us voted against Turk, we were on his blacklist and Rourke's, too. There was no way they'd cooperate with us.

Rourke was odd and could be especially nasty if he didn't get his way. A good-looking guy, a bit like Jack Kennedy, with red wavy hair, medium build, about average height. He had a reputation; in the community we called him "Slapsy," because he was always kind of off the wall. We just thought he was kind of whacky. I remember when I was in the eighth grade, Rourke announced that he was going to take his car motor apart and put it all back together again in the park. A group of us went to watch the spectacle. He did exactly what he said he would: he took it all apart and put it all back together again. It was to demonstrate his hyper-intellect. He was also the guy who would stay awake for three days.

I never really saw him again after that until around 1962, when he told my mother he was interested in getting involved with our group. After the election, it seemed he couldn't accept that he couldn't manipulate us. He thought he could outsmart anyone. He was smart, no doubt about that. He got his master's degree in physics from RPI and worked as a nuclear technician for Knolls Atomic Power Laboratory.

It was even stranger because I never had a bad word with him. In fact, I had supported him and helped run his campaign. I think he didn't like that I was winning tough challenges by working hard and strategizing, not just going off-the-cuff like he would, and unlike him, I was well known and well liked in town.

One day, shortly before the election, Jim Kellogg, Campaign Manager in the First Ward, told me a story about Rourke. Rourke told Jim, "If Van Buskirk were standing in a puddle of gasoline, I'd throw a match in it."

Jim said, "You might blow yourself up."

Rourke responded, "It'd be worth it."

I believed Jim. He was a friend and a pretty honest guy. He had no reason to tell tall tales. I knew then, boy, I got problems with this guy, Rourke. He wanted to be the leader and the center of everything.

Curran could also be difficult, but I had a lot of respect for him. He had been a naval officer in World War II, and had graduated from RPI with a degree in metallurgy. He was clever and analytical. He worked as a manager at General Electric. He was stubborn; his mother used to say about him that if he did not get what he wanted, he'd pick up his marbles and go home, even if it ruined the game for everyone else. He was always concerned about his reputation, and I would ask, "What about our reputations?" He was a commanding speaker. He had presence: he was a tall and a little overweight, had thin brown hair, and wore glasses. He made the perfect bureaucrat. He always had to hold meetings. It would drive me nuts. We used to say he had to have meetings to plan his meetings. Still, we had worked well together during the many budget hearings.

Bob seemed to resent me. If he ever heard anyone say, "Paul's doing a great job," Bob would say, "No one is indispensable." He said that all the time.

Bob would pontificate and claim he had the moral high ground, while Rourke thought he was the smartest guy in the room and therefore should get all the power, but it was Dr. Harry who was becoming the real skunk at the lawn party. He wanted one of his brothers for building inspector and another for the first mayor's appointment to the school board. Fortunately however, Dr. Jay appointed members of the School Improvement Committee to the school board.

For the most part, all of the appointees were good ones: Frank Landry, law clerk to Supreme Court Justice Ellis Staley, as our police court justice, and Stanton Ablett, a former city court judge, for our corporation counsel with Carl Engstrom, as his deputy. John Percy, my professor at RPI was the city engineer. Tom Donnelly, a local CPA, was city comptroller. Bob Curran was Common Council President. Lastly, Irene Rivet, a retired executive assistant, was city clerk.

Once everyone was assigned a role, Jay put together teams of his new city department heads to work with the outgoing ones to help with the transition. I was never assigned a team, so I didn't participate. According to Carl Engstrom, that was because the committee was afraid it would look like I was taking over as a political boss, like Dawson.

I knew I was being pushed out. Even though I had been the one to start the momentum of change in town, the old doubts about whether I should stay in Cohoes or move south crept back in. Already I had observed that when certain people got elected, they begin acting strangely. Before the election, they would pretend to be everybody's friend. After the election, they would think, "I've got power. I know more than everybody knows."

Bob Curran and Frank Rourke were like that. Turk just wanted easy money, and Rourke liked having Turk around because he was easy to manipulate. Carl and Harry wanted power over everyone else.

I started to feel uneasy. There were going to be serious problems in governing. But I didn't rush in with my concerns. I decided to wait and see, just like with the canoes at camp.

CHAPTER NINETEEN:

1964 INAUGURAL HEADACHES

Inauguration day should have been a day of celebration after a hard-fought victory. Instead, almost immediately after the election, the seeds of infighting were being sown.

Harry told me several weeks after the election that he thought Rourke was a genius. Meanwhile, Rourke and Turk were promoting the narrative that I was a political boss like Dawson, and that it had been okay for me to run the campaign but not to run City Hall. Harold would say to me, "They are looking for a sheep to slaughter to purify themselves."

Brady, Dr. Jay's appointee, had created chaos for the Fusion Party, another third political party during the 1930s, when he was corporation counsel. He was a brilliant trial attorney; however, no law firm would have him, so he worked alone from home. He believed his mission was to deliver the Citizens Party to Dan O'Connell.

Meanwhile, Dawson was promoting his own narrative, telling his supporters that he would be back in four years. He averred that the Citizens Party did not know how to govern, that there would be so much infighting that many of our people would join his side, and that city employees would not cooperate with the new administration.

I worried that he wasn't wrong. I was tired after four years of fighting the Machine, especially after the election. Now I had members of my own party who wanted to diminish my role in carrying out our promises. I was not only physically tired, but also emotionally exhausted; I didn't want to go to the ceremonies. In the end, I decided that it was important that I be there.

The ceremony and swearing-in were in the afternoon in the large hallway on the first floor. The Democratic elected officials had declined our invitation to attend the ceremony and had been sworn in that morning. Rourke was running around like he was in charge. I left after taking the oath as an assessor.

The next day, Dr. Jay asked Turk for the keys to City Hall. Turk refused. He said that since he was responsible for the security of the building, he would be the one to let people in and out. The mayor told him, "If I don't have that key in two hours, you're fired."

When we finally took office, the place was in chaos. Nobody knew where to go to, what to do, or where to start. Before taking office, Dr. Jay sent a letter to Santspree and all of his department heads with a copy to the state attorney general. The letter warned the mayor against the unlawful removal or destruction of city records. Dr. Jay also requested that Santspree have each department inventory all their supplies and equipment. Santspree did not reply to either letter.

Soon, we learned that since the election, the assessed property values for the Machine party faithful had been drastically reduced, resulting in thousands of missed tax revenue, and that Santspree had ordered the removal of all parking meters. He'd also issued a tax anticipation note on any upcoming tax revenues for the year to pay all outstanding city bills. This meant that we would start fiscal year 1964 in the hole.

As other irregularities and Machine era legacies began to surface, I realized that there were more problems to be solved than we expected, and that because of my experience, I was the one who knew how to solve them.

CHAPTER TWENTY

ANOTHER GAME OF CHESS

One of the first things we did was to look at the tax assessment rolls. I suspected that Dawson had fiddled with them. Bob Curran, Harold Reavey, Frank Rourke, and a couple of other Citizens Party members had all had their property values raised. It hardly seemed like a coincidence.

Meanwhile, the assessments on two of Santspree's properties and on Dawson's home had been lowered. Overall, they had lowered the assessments on 80 properties, causing a loss of $176,000 in revenues. We restored the highly political assessments and left the rest alone for the time being. In addition, Santspree's order to have all the parking meters removed before the start of our term had left us $20,000 short.

Meanwhile, we had discovered $86,253 worth of unpaid city bills . Dr. Jay told me that the debts might be as high as $94,000. He was wrong. They eventually reached $180,000 and dated back to 1960.

Taken together, we began our operations $375,000 shy of a $1.3 million budget. We would have to raise the property tax rate substantially, giving Dawson the chance to call us amateurs unable to manage the city—and the potential for some people to agree with him.

It got worse. Before leaving, the Dawsoncrats in the Common Council had passed a $50,000 bond issue for a garbage collection contract, awarding it to Carl Newell. I was determined to make this grand scheme backfire on Dawson. We hired Paul Coughlin as special counsel to our corporation counsel. He asked the State Supreme Court for a restraining order to prevent the award and bond issue. The court ruled in our favor.

Bob Curran and I drafted the budget with input from all the department heads. Because of our experience analyzing Santspree's budgets over the previous four years, we knew where the fat was and how to cut it. We were able to reduce the cost of operations by $100,000. Next, we would need to present it to the Board of Estimate and Apportionment. Once reviewed and possibly revised, it would go to the Common Council at a public hearing. We were sure it would play to a full house, and it did.

Santspree was there with his entourage, only now they were behind the wooden railing, just as the early Citizens Committee had been in 1960. We were now the ones on the dais. The audience had been transformed over the years, too. Now it was made up of interested voters, standing room only, instead of the city employees who'd been mandated to attend (until being mandated not to attend).

Santspree was presenting his proposed 1964 budget, which included items addressing all the issues we'd pointed out during the campaign, all the things he'd failed to do over the previous four years. He called for $14 per $1,000 of assessed value tax increases to cover all his suggested improvements.

Our proposed budget included salary raises for the police force, fire fighters, City Hall clerks, and public works employees, along with health insurance and participation in the state retirement plan. We were sure to include a line item to hire an outside auditor to audit the city's finances. There was an item for unpaid bills for $80,000, which we now knew had reached $180,000.

Santspree told the crowd that doing so amounted to "double taxation." Bob Curran replied, "We would be glad to hand these bills back to you."

Santspree got tired of sparring with Bob Curran and of heckling from the audience. He confessed that the figures used in his proposed budget were not his responsibility. "They're estimated expenses submitted to me by my department heads. I merely turned the recommendations over to the new administration," he said.

When it came time to vote, our budget passed 4 to 3, with the three Democrats on the council voting as a bloc. Alderman Emma Shea called our budget an "absurdity," Albert Skawinski called it "a farce," and James Daley, the third Democrat, called it an "unlawful expenditure of funds."

CHAPTER TWENTY-ONE

IN THROUGH THE WINDOW

We had to get rid of the Dawsoncrats still crawling all over City Hall. With them around, Dawson effectively maintained control over the Civil Service Commission, giving him the power to undermine us left and right. If we did not stabilize City Hall, the chaos would never end.

I went to Carl Engstrom, our deputy corporation counsel. "We've got to get rid of those guys on the Civil Service Commission," I told him.

He said, "No, there's nothing you can do. You have to wait until their terms are up."

Now, wait a minute, I was thinking. These guys were serving a six-year term, and Dawson's brother-in-law, Bill Fuss, was the Chairman of the Civil Service Commission and controlled who got hired. We couldn't hire anybody without going through the commission. So, the score was that here we were in office, but Dawson still controlled the personnel.

"We'll be out of office by then," I said to Engstrom. He just shrugged it off, which raised my suspicions about him.

So I went to Paul Coughlin. "Paul, we've got to get rid of the guys on the Civil Service Commission."

"Oh yeah. We can do that," he replied.

"What have we got to do?"

"We've got to bring them up on charges," Paul he said casually.

"How do we do that?"

He said, "If we have a look at their files, I'm sure we can find things in there that we can charge them with."

I was thinking, how are we going to do that? Fuss came to work every day, and he wasn't about to give us a peek at his files. He locked the door every night and whenever he went out. Not even the janitors had the chance to clean his office. It was like Fort Knox.

I asked Paul, "Well, can't we claim there's smoke coming under the door, and we had to break it down because of fire?"

"No, no," he said. "Paul, that won't work."

I kept thinking about it. One day, I was over at the post office, right across the street from City Hall, looking up at the second floor. There were huge windows up there. I could see the locks on the windows—they were unlocked. If I got myself on the ledge, I could inch over, open the window, and get into Fuss's office.

That Sunday night, Coughlin was in City Hall. Nobody else was around. Bill Riley had given me his key to the recreation department office, which was right next to the Civil Service Commission. I let myself into Bill's office, opened one of those huge windows, and stepped out on the ledge. The ledge was maybe about a foot wide. I pressed myself spread-eagled against the building, one side of my face against the stone, and shuffled over to the commission's window. I opened it and I stepped inside.

Coughlin was waiting for me outside the commission's door. I let him in. There was a file cabinet, but it had a lock-bar around it. Easy enough: we just took the bar off with a screwdriver. We pulled out all the files. Coughlin and I went through them, pulled out all the stuff we wanted, copied them, and put them all back in their place. We closed all the doors and windows and headed home. Nice and tidy.

The next morning, Coughlin had his secretary type up a long list of charges against Bill Fuss and the other commissioners. Then he had the police to deliver them to Fuss's office. We had the evidence Fuss's people had been cheating on all the exams, giving them to people in advance, handing out jobs to people who didn't qualify, keeping people on the list of potential hires even after they'd flunked the exam more than four times. The law mandated that if someone failed it four times, they were out. Just as I'd known all along, these guys were keeping unqualified people around and then reclassifying their jobs. Luckily for us, they were dumb enough to keep good records on all this. It was a mess.

Within two hours, all the commissioners were in the city clerk's office, handing in their resignations. That was the end of that.

Dr. Jay appointed his own commissioners, reformers. They elected Frank Bourgeois, a reformer, as their Secretary. He did a terrific job. Frank brought in the State Commission to administer and grade the exams. It worked. If there was an opening for a policeman, a fireman, or clerk, he'd advertise it in the paper. People applied and took the exam. If there were three or more that passed the exam, then the department head could pick one of the three. We never had any complaints or accusations of unfair hiring. If they passed the exam, they were a candidate. We did that for the next four years. We followed the law, and it worked.

CHAPTER TWENTY-TWO

CALMING THE CHAOS: DELIVERING ON PROMISES

While on the surface it appeared things were going well, by March, there was still chaos. The Democrats' policy was to obstruct us whenever they could. Since the Common Council was split along party lines, Dr. Jay would usually end up casting the deciding vote.

Many of the city departments were operating in their own silos. When they had a problem, they did not know where to go or what to do. I can understand how some reform groups that win in local elections fail to get a second term, depending on their learning curve and the amount of resistance from within.

I will admit that the Public Works Department was among our best performing departments, doing a good job with snow removal, spring clean-up, and general street maintenance, but that wasn't thanks to Turk Senecal. He had no experience and no leadership skills. It was Art Defruscio, a long-time department employee, who was taking care of business while Turk was busy politicking and stoking his fires with the Democratic aldermen. He was betting on their returning to power and wanted to stay in their good graces.

Turk was trying to build his own empire, coalescing with Engstrom, Rourke, and Harry. Each had their own agenda, which united them in a way, since it meant none of them had prioritized doing what was best for the city. Rourke was encouraging Dr. Marra to do a citywide reassessment. On top of the assessment intrigue, Dawson and Santspree had left us with low residential assessments and high commercial assessments. If we did a reassessment this early in our administration, we would have to raise residential assessments for the people who voted and lower commercial ones. That would wreak political havoc, and I think Rourke and Dr. Harry knew it.

Dr. Jay was busy chairing the Common Council, the Board of Estimate and Apportionment, and the Contract and Supply department, as well as attending many social events and running his medical practice. He was aware that his strength was being among people, not managing them. He needed someone to coordinate the various departments, commissions, and boards to achieve the goals and objectives we had outlined during our campaign. He asked me to take on this role and titled it "city administrator."

Bob Curran did not like that one bit. As the council's President, he told the Board of Estimate and Apportionment to create the position but to call it "executive secretary to the mayor." The duties were the same: manage the day-to-day operations of the city and carry out the Citizens Party agenda. I took the job and resigned from my teaching position in the civil technology department of Hudson Valley Community College. The title didn't matter to me. I only wanted to get the job done.

Engstrom was angry when he heard I'd accepted the job. He began openly accusing me of being a political boss, just like Dawson.

I wasn't a boss. I was a professional urban planner and civil engineer whose skills were needed for the city. What was Engstrom talking about? Dawson also had called me a political boss during the campaign, but that was dirt as usual. This was coming from my own team. I kept my mouth shut, but I started to watch my back.

Once I took the position and could start systematizing all the departments, putting the right people in the right places, things started to calm down. The four years we'd spent as advocates of good government had prepared us well. We understood the city charter. We could analyze the city's finances against a backdrop of historical knowledge about the city's issues, making it easier to implement our platform and address the issues of the campaign.

That year, we applied for several federal and state grants, planned and sought funding for a new central fire station, revamped the planning commission, created a new parks and recreation commission, reinstalled the parking meters, passed local laws to provide for better fiscal practices, partnered with the New York State Division of Standards and Purchases to get better deals on any necessary equipment and supplies, and developed a tense but productive relationship with the Common Council.

Dr. Jay had Paul Coughlin draw up mismanagement charges against Matty Grestini, the recreation department's director under Santspree. We used the documentation from our report on the condition of the parks in 1963 for the specific charges. Dr. Jay appointed a board for the new parks and recreation commission; Bill Riley was elected its Chairman. Bill recruited staff, laid out a strategic plan for rebuilding programs and the parks, per our campaign promise, and took a week off from work to get the city swimming pool in operating condition. He set up programs throughout the city, including storytelling, skiing, ice hockey, volleyball, basketball, and a citywide doll contest, among many others.

It was part of our campaign promise to obtain and fill the polluted canals where more than a dozen children had drowned over the years. Our promise had been to purchase the canals and, using state and federal aid, construct sewer intercepts, ultimately turning them into an improved, citywide system of parks and playgrounds.

In July, I started negotiations with Niagara Mohawk Power Company to acquire the power canals no longer used by the mills. At that time, sewerage emptied into the canals from various points throughout the city. Niagara Mohawk wanted us to take over the canals for $1. I wouldn't agree to that. I wanted them to pay for the pipe and fill in Canal #1 for a park and playground in the First Ward, to accomplish one of our promises. Eventually, they agreed to fill in Canal #1 and the city purchased them for $1. The canals also provided a natural right of way for future sewer intercepts at no cost.

In September, we started negotiations with the state to fill in the Champlain Canal, which ran the length of three-quarters of the city on a North–South axis. Whereas the power canals would intercept one-third of the city sewage, the Champlain Canal would intercept the other two-thirds.

At this time, cities were dumping raw sewerage into the Hudson and Mohawk Rivers. To help reverse the levels of pollution the rivers had reached, the federal and state governments would allocate funds to pay 83.33% of the cost to plan and construct sewer intercepts and treatment plants along the Mohawk and Hudson Rivers. We filed applications and received approval for funding. The Democrats on the council opposed our canals and wastewater initiative. They even took us to court. This may have been a smart move if they wanted to stay in Dawson's good graces, but politically, it was foolish, which soon became apparent.

Meanwhile, I had my own little sewer project to attend to. One day, Jenny, the mayor's secretary, told me that there was an elderly gentleman named John Byron who wanted to see me. I used to see him around and would say hi to him. He'd told her that back in the 1930s he'd been the city engineer. He had read in the paper that I was a graduate of RPI, his alma mater. When I came out of my office to meet him, he seemed to teeter on his feet. I think he had been drinking, but it could have been because he was already in his eighties.

He had a map of some of the city water lines rolled up under his arm. He offered it to me for $1. I bought it and thanked him. That wasn't the last of it. Mr. Byron kept coming back nearly each week for months, each time offering me a different map of the city's water and sewer lines, for a dollar a piece. I'm sure each of his visits was preceded by a trip to the local pub.

When I told John Brady about it, he told me John Byron had been with him in the administration back in the 1930s. Brady remembered some story he'd heard about how whenever Byron had wanted a reason to leave City Hall for the day to go for a drink, he would roll up a map of the water or sewer systems and go to the local pub. He'd stay there all day, and then when he'd go home at night, he'd put the maps under his bed. It took me a $100 of my own money and a year to get all the maps back.

Shortly after we took office, the School Improvement Group sent a letter to the school board members, asking them to resign so Dr. Jay could appoint new members. Naturally, they refused, saying the letter was an insult. Over the course of the next year, as various school board members' terms expired, Dr. Jay appointed Jim Bottum, an analyst with the state Department of Taxation and Finance, and Millie Freije. Santspree's three other appointees decided to throw in with us and elected Jim Bottum President of the board. School reform could begin at last.

If not statewide, thanks to the governor, then we could at least make a difference in Cohoes now that we had enough votes on the Common Council to authorize a local ordinance allowing the creation and circulation of a petition to elect a school board. The referendum ultimately passed.

In October, the school board with Dr. Jay's newly appointed reformers purchased a site for construction of a new high school to help ease overcrowding. Several of the old elementary schools were condemned and would be combined into one. We were starting to deliver on our campaign promises.

CHAPTER TWENTY-THREE

GOING TO SEE THE POPE

Being granted a meeting with Dan O'Connell was like being granted an audience with the Pope. I think that is why Dr. Jay agreed to meet with him. He was a curiosity. Virginia told me I needed to go, too.

I said, "Virginia, I haven't been invited. I don't want to go."

She refused to let me out of it. "I'll see that you get an invitation. I'm just worried Jay might say something that he should not." A few days later, she called me up, "You have your invitation. You're going there with Jay." I don't know how she pulled it off, but she did.

O'Connell was a kind of puppet master, but like Mike Smith, he knew how to make people feel welcome. I felt right at home the first time I met him, even though I didn't really want to be there. This was in 1964, several months after we had been elected into office. John Brady and William Morrissey were also present. Brady had never hidden the fact that he was a friend of Dan. Morrissey, who had been the commissioner of public safety during the Fusion administration in the 1930s when his brother John was mayor. William and John Morrissey, along with Brady, had all sold out to O'Connell. Still, I was surprised to see Morrissey there, since he'd been out of the game all those years.

I was the odd one out. I didn't know what the purpose of the meeting was. I don't think there was one. Brady had arranged it. It was likely that he wanted to play the power broker role, to show that he could deliver the Citizens Party to Dan O'Connell.

We met at Dan's house in Albany. It was a modest home in a modest neighborhood. He had a parrot on his shoulder and a couple of big dogs lying around. Before we started the meeting, Dan caged the parrot and draped a cover over it, perhaps so it would not repeat conversations.

By now, all the Citizens Party people elected to the county legislature were raising hell with O'Connell's people, especially Ralph Robinson. Ralph was calling for an investigation into Dan's county officials and their business dealings. At the meeting, Brady kept telling Dan, "Now, Jay and Paul here, they're not with this Ralph Robinson guy." Dan looked at him and said calmly, "Robinson can make all the noise he wants. I don't care. I got the votes."

It was a non-event. O'Connell was short on talk with us. It was more interesting to me to see Uncle Dan with his two nieces when they came running into the room. They had just come back from Europe, according to Dan. They ran in, he hugged and kissed them, and then they took off again. After the nieces, in came Mayor Corning. He ran down the list of agendas for the Albany City Council. He talked about this and that ordinance to be proposed, giving them to Dan to review before the council voted on it. I think O'Connell let Corning run the show as long as he kept that direct line of communication.

I also think O'Connell spent a lot of time reading. He was a sports fan, especially baseball. He didn't spend the day running the party; the party mostly ran itself. He had confidence in people the people around him. He had institutionalized his program and was just letting it run. He had plenty of other activities to keep his attention. He owned a beer business, for example: Hedrick beer. It was horrible beer, but the bars had to buy it to win their patronage with the Machine. Bar owners would buy it and then put the keg in the backroom. No one would actually think of drinking the stuff.

We had a second meeting later that same year. It was up at Dan's summer place in the Heidelberg Mountains. It was a camp with no running water; instead, it had a pump for the well.

This time, it was Dr. Jay, Bob Curran, Frank Colaruotolo, John Brady, William Morrissey, and me in attendance. By now, Lyndon Johnson was running for President against Barry Goldwater, and Bobby Kennedy was running to be New York State's U.S. Senator. Brady was going on about how we had to have a Citizens Party for Johnson campaign. Johnson needed our vote like he needed a hole in his head. Everyone knew he was going to cream Goldwater. I was thinking, why the hell did we have to have a special meeting about this? We were useless to Johnson. But Brady ranted on and on and on. It was getting boring. I found a newspaper lying there, so I ignored everybody and started reading it. Then I heard Bob Curran say, "I think we ought to have a group, Citizens for Bobby Kennedy." He was talking in his holier-than-thou voice.

I knew that Joe Kennedy and Dan O'Connell were good friends, so it caught my attention when O'Connell said to Curran, "Bobby's a no-good son of a bitch."

Curran didn't know what to do. O'Connell made a disgusted face and quipped, "He called me when he wanted to run for the Senate here, and I told him to have his father call me." Then he added, "When his brother, Jack, wanted to run for president, the first person who called me was his father. He called and asked me to support him."

Curran didn't say another word the whole time.

At one point, I asked for a drink of water. O'Connell said, "Sure. Come with me." He led me out to the back of the house where the well was. He said, "This is good, fresh water. You're going to like this water."

I got a drink, and it was cold and refreshing.

"You know, you're the only smart one in there. You're reading the paper. You're probably learning something."

Maybe now I could say I had had a drink with Dan O'Connell.

CHAPTER TWENTY-FOUR

PAID ONCE, WILL BE PAID AGAIN

Dawson might have thought they were leaving us holding the bag for their unpaid bills, but it gave us the perfect opportunity to crack down on the Machine's corruption. We hired independent auditors in February, and by May, the auditors discovered that Santspree's administration had paid a 100% markup to purchase traffic signals and equipment from Albany Equipment and Supply. That happened to be one of the companies in Dan O'Connell's pocket and a target for investigation by Governor Dewey in 1943. Now Cohoes would launch its own investigation.

According to the city charter, the comptroller had the power to subpoena people when settling a claim. So, that's exactly what Tom Donnelly, our city comptroller and a non-Dawsoncrat Democrat did. He scheduled hearings, which began in May. Paul Coughlin represented the city.

The first hearing examined why Albany Equipment and Supply had been so overpaid. Coughlin asked Mrs. Gaul, the firm's bookkeeper, if she thought a 100% markup was fair. "It is if you don't know whether or not you are actually going to get paid," she said.

Coughlin pointed out one discrepancy after another. There were entries for chemicals designated for the water treatment plant that were never delivered. There were entries for traffic lights sold at a 100% markup and a host of other items that were never delivered, never installed, or sold at twice the price.

Matty Grestini, Director of Recreation, testified that he made purchases from Albany Equipment and Supply for baseballs, bats, gloves, and catcher's equipment without knowing the price. This was a typical example of the machine's preferred vendors with no public bidding. Employees of the city's treasury department testified that nearly all city checks for vendors were picked up by Eddie Clark or Edward Colozza, two of Dawson's henchmen. The press reported that Coughlin wove a "convincing case" against the purchasing practices of the prior administration.

The second hearing was in June. Carl Newell had an unpaid claim for $82,751. Newell was one of Dawson's favorite contractors: he was the one who'd gotten all the "emergency bids," which were really no-bid contracts. The day of the hearing, Coughlin stopped by my office before going up to the Council Chamber.

"Jesus, Paul, I don't know what I'm going to do today. I don't have anything on Newell. I don't know what I'm going to do."

I asked him if he would like to have Carl Newell's books. "What? Hell yes!" he said.

I handed them over.

He couldn't believe it. "Where did you get these?" he asked.

I told him they were sitting in a neat little package outside my door when I got in that morning. He pawed through them, grabbed the books, and took off upstairs.

Now, at that time, I wasn't about to tell Coughlin, or anybody, where I'd gotten those books, but here's where they came from. I usually got into the office early. The papers had been thoroughly covering the hearings. Everyone knew Newell was up next. So early that morning, in came Paul Taglioni. He had the city's contract to haul garbage. He did a great job, and there were never any complaints against him.

When he entered the office, he got straight to the point, "Paul, would you like to have Newell's books?"

I didn't hesitate, "Yes. Yes, I would."

He went out to his car, came back, and gave me an accordion file of all of Newell's books. I don't know how the hell he got them. I think he and Newell had some kind of under-the-table deal going before having a falling-out. I wasn't about to question it.

So, Paul Coughlin faced off against Newell in the hearing. As soon as Newell swore in, Paul pulled out the books.

"Mr. Newell, can you read this here?"

Newell looked where Coughlin's pointing. It was for an item attributed to the City of Cohoes.

Newell refused to read it, so Coughlin read it out loud instead, "Was paid once, will be paid again."

There were a whole lot of entries like that. Coughlin read them all aloud. Newell pleaded the Fifth Amendment.

The hits kept coming. Over the summer, the auditors analyzed the Santspree administration's handling of the Manor Heights Storm water and street project. The city engineer had estimated the cost would be exactly $77,125. The city had received three bids, including one that came in under the estimate by about $5,000. The auditors found that Santspree's Board of Contract and Supply rejected the bid as being too high. Instead, the city hired the Cohoes Construction Company, another of Dawson's favorite contractors that had gone bankrupt and had to change its name. In addition to paying the company to rent and repair the Cohoes Construction Company's backhoe, the company had been hired to construct thirteen manholes when it should have built twenty. The auditors estimated that just over half of the project had been completed and at a cost $81,261. Santspree let Dawson give the rebuttal to that one. Dawson said 95% of the project had been completed before we had taken office.

I went to the site with a surveyor's instrument to measure line and grade and checked all the elevations of the manholes, catch basins, and storm pipes. They were a mess. I had to redesign the project to drain properly and decided it wasn't even worth the bother to have the contractors fix it. Instead, I had our Department of Public Works finish the project.

We also took legal action against Leo Santini, a local general contractor, for collecting fourteen payments of about $800 each for rental of certain trucks and drivers that were allegedly never supplied in 1963. We also filed suit against Newell to get back nearly $4,000 in over-payments.

The auditors' final report concluded that the previous administration had engaged in improper purchasing procedures, preferential vendor treatment, unnecessary city expenditures, mis-application of protocols, and insufficient internal controls.

Albany Equipment and Supply were suing the city to recover payment for their bills. After a lot of back and forth, we ultimately won the case in the State Court of Appeals. The judge asked Paul Coughlin if he planned to refer the case for criminal prosecution. Paul said he would take it under advisement. We knew that O'Connell's district attorney would never prosecute, so we settled for our comptroller, Donnelly, to declare approximately $100,000 of the claims were not legitimate, and therefore we did not have to pay them.

CHAPTER TWENTY-FIVE

WHO'S THE BOSS?

That summer, Rourke was still going on about doing a city-wide assessment. He hadn't stopped since the day we entered City Hall. We didn't do it because I knew it would ruin us and told Dr. Jay as much. After decades of Democratic control, most of the commercial properties in town were over-assessed, and most of the residential ones were under-assessed. A new assessment would mean a sudden, drastic rise in taxes on residents. It would have been like ripping off the bandage before the wound had healed. We needed to earn the trust of the voters by showing them we would fulfill our campaign promises. They needed to know we could run the city competently before we told them it would cost them more personally. Already we had to raise taxes to pay for the shortage created by the previous administration. A citywide assessment would have been a stake through the heart.

As far as the assessments were concerned, as long as we didn't use them punitively like the Machine had, we were ahead of the game, and of course we weren't going to do that, so it was a moot point. I tried to explain this to Rourke, but he wanted the glory for crusading against corruption. Give it time, I told him. We were already reversing decades of corruption through the independent auditors and civil hearings. Dr. Jay agreed with me. Rourke was furious.

Rourke redoubled his accusations that I was a political boss. Anyone who'd listen got an earful about how I should not have a position in City Hall because I was still Chair of the Citizens Party. I saw the subtext to Carl Engstrom's, our Deputy Corporation

Counsel, warning: be good at campaigning, be good at policy and administration, but don't be both or else we can say you're just trying to be the boss. It sounded sensible, until you thought about it for half a second and realized that I wasn't choosing the appointments. I wasn't penalizing people with assessments. I wasn't misappropriating funds. What I was doing was being a successful professional and applying my skills as a city planner and engineer in the service of solving our community's problems, which was what thrilled me most.

Rourke had started scheming with the other unhappy fellows, Senecal and Dr. Harry. Harry had several siblings, mostly brothers. I think some of them saw his election as an opportunity to get in on the action. One of them, Jim, a pharmacist, had been a school board appointee under Mike Smith. When Dewey set about investigating the Cohoes arm of the Albany Machine, Jim plead guilty to a misdemeanor: he'd been selling pharmaceutical supplies to the school but never quite got around to delivering them after he'd been paid.

Harry wanted Jim appointed to the school board and one of his other brothers to be the building inspector. Dr. Jay asked me what I thought. I told him we already had plenty of people in town who'd fought on behalf of the School Improvement Committee and who had brought about actual change. Why not appoint one of them, I suggested.

Harry was furious. He'd lost face with his brother, and now he blamed me. He and Rourke started telling people I was against their plans to make tax assessments fairer. They said that Dr. Jay and I were no different than the Dawsoncrats.

In early October, the Board of Estimate and Apportionment announced that it had officially established a position for the executive secretary to the mayor, which I gladly took. I had been working as the "acting" executive secretary, without pay, since March. Jim Kellogg was elected to my place as tax assessor.

Bob Curran had gotten his way: I was not an administrator. This meant I would have no statutory power at all. My only power lay in my good relationship with the mayor. The Board set my annual salary at $9,000, comparable to other city administrators of similar sized cities. That's when the fun began.

The Troy Record reported it was the highest salary ever paid to a Cohoes city official, which was incorrect. Dr. Herrick Conners, the do-nothing superintendent of our public schools, was paid $12,125 annually.

Harry made his move. My new salary was good cover for his long-festering, insidious intent. He told the paper, "My attempt to take assessments out of politics just is not working out. It is still being used as a political football." He also made a sideways accusation that we were as corrupt as or more corrupt than Dawson's people. "The very thing we were trying to lick is back, only bigger," he told reporters.

When the question of replacing Marra was raised with the Council, Rourke made his own move. He nominated William Ryan, former deputy corporate counsel under Santspree, to fill the term of elected assessor. Naturally, the three Democrats on the council were delighted, doubly so when Rourke joined with them to vote Ryan in.

Rourke released a statement afterward, "I do not believe in the present dangerous arrangement whereby the chairman of the Citizens Committee also occupies the position of extreme influence in City Hall." He added he would do whatever it took to, "block the actions of anyone seeking undue power."

Then he held a meeting in his home hosting the six district leaders of the Citizens Party in his ward. He reiterated his opposition to "bossism."

"I am a member of the Democratic Party," Rourke announced. "The Citizens Committee is only a statement of principles on which we agreed to run." He accused the Citizens Party of abandoning its principals by paying me $9,000 a year. Rourke knew it would be unreasonable to expect someone to execute a full-time position without pay, and that competitive salaries attract experience candidates.

The party's district leaders unanimously tossed Rourke out as ward leader and voted in a new one, right there in Rourke's own house. The official reason they gave was that they could not support the nomination and election of William Ryan, which was true, but unofficially, none of them understood or trusted Rourke. At best he was a turncoat; at worst he was delusional.

Next, the Citizens Party organization of each ward met. They coordinated a letter to the editor of *The Troy Record* stating their support for the mayor. They endorsed my appointment and salary. Most of all, they refuted Rourke's latest claims that the Party was divided.

It was a month of shake-ups. Bob Boivin had just resigned as treasurer two days before. The paper reported that it was because he had been offered a well-paying sales job further upstate but intimated that internal politics among the Citizens was the real reason he wanted out. I think Rourke had been pestering Bob, and because he didn't want to get involved in the conflict, he decided to get out altogether.

I resigned as party chairman, not because of the accusations from Rourke or Harry, but because my duties as executive secretary to the mayor were time-consuming, and frankly, I was more excited about that role. The last thing in the world I needed was to be chairman of the party. It's a thankless job having to keep everyone happy and in the loop. On top of that, there was no upcoming election to manage, and everyone from our party was operating aboveboard. There were no fires to put out or battles to wage. So

I was happy to resign as chairman of the party. Bob Curran was elected to succeed me.

A brief postscript to that: a year or so later, the party wanted me to run again. Bob himself, who had also made claims of bossism against me, nominated me and praised me for being a great chairman. I accepted only because I was voted back in unanimously, and I did not want to let the party down.

CHAPTER TWENTY-SIX

A VERY GOOD YEAR

It was touch and go with Dr. Jay; you never knew what kind of mood he was going to be in or if he was going to stay focused. We got along pretty well, though. I understood him. As mayor, he had a lot of tough decisions to make, and he trusted me to give him a straight answer if he asked. He supported me in all that I did, too.

A few people, like Bob Curran, didn't like Dr. Jay, though. They didn't understand how to work with his flightiness and wanted him to be more executive-like. Curran didn't get it: Dr. Jay was there to be the icon, the face of our movement, and I was there behind the scenes to administrate, handling the details that were beyond Dr. Jay.

The politicking behind the scenes did not stop us from getting things done. In August, the Common Council voted to establish the Cohoes Economic Opportunity Commission as part of President Johnson's War on Poverty. There were ten members of the commission, all appointed by Dr. Jay. Cohoes was the first municipality in the capital region to sign on to this federal program, which made grants covering up to 90% of the cost of eligible projects. To help the city maximize every potential federal dollar, the planning commission hired a consultant to create a comprehensive plan—a prerequisite for federal and state funding—for urban renewal, code enforcement, housing, historic preservation, and a host of other aspects of town planning. In the end, the federal government paid two-thirds of the cost of the plan, and the state paid one-sixth. Under this program, I also applied for federal and state funds to build a new central fire station that would include a county emergency operating center.

In our first year, we could now point to a solid list of promises fulfilled. In addition to having secured state funds for a comprehensive planning program, we had gotten rid of Dawson's recreation director and Civil Service Commission and exposed his corrupt purchasing practices.

As I mentioned earlier, we had negotiated an agreement with Niagara Mohawk Power to acquire the fetid power canals. At the time, the canals were not only a drowning risk but also basically open sewers. When the water was stagnant, the stench was nauseating. If we were to be a modern community, we needed to fill them in. We had federal and state grants for water pollution control to complete our study of the cost of sewer intercepts and wastewater treatment, so we could now apply for millions of dollars of federal and state grants to construct the project to eliminate and treat our system of open sewers.

We were now participating in the state's retirement system and implemented new training programs for police and firemen, while giving raises and medical insurance to city employees.

Another task was getting rid of the Police Chief, a Dawson appointee who could not pass the Civil Service exam, and who had no leadership skills or administrative experience. His name was Harold Smith. As a detective, he had tried to smear the reputation of a seventeen-year-old kid whose uncle had helped to get Mike Smith indicted. I was assigned to call him into my office to tell him that it was in his best interest to resign.

Those of us who truly were reformers had accomplished much. I would say that, aside from Dr. Jay and myself, that group included Bob Curran as President of the City Council, Frank Colaruotolo as President pro tempore, Bill Riley running parks and recreation, Frank Bourgeois in civil service, Stanton Ablett and

Paul Coughlin as the corporation counsels, Tom Donnelly in the comptroller's office, Frank Landry at police court, Bill Corbett in the treasurer's office, Irene Rivet at the city clerk's office, and Ralph Robinson heading the Planning Commission. Also committed to reform were our new school board members, who finally got rid of the corrupt and inept superintendent, a peacock of a man who did nothing but strut in and out of our classrooms, demanding that students sing good morning to him. Now, we could hire a young, progressive superintendent to run the schools.

Politics over policy was still a big concern, however. Now that Rourke had alienated himself from the Citizens Party, the danger was that he would align himself with the Democrats. He had already publicly pledged his allegiance to them, despite being elected on the Citizens ticket. Power players like Turk were running public works; the Housing Authority was still controlled by the Machine, while the assessor's office was neutral.

Soon we would see how this would play out: it was time to prepare for the budget meeting for the following year.

CHAPTER TWENTY-SEVEN

CALM BEFORE THE STORM: 1965

The 1965 budget called for a dollar decrease in the tax rate and provided for increases in salaries for the police and firemen, increases in the purchase of equipment for recreation, matching funds for the planning commission's comprehensive plan, and data processing equipment. Revenues included $67,000 from the federal government for the War on Poverty programs. Surprisingly, the budget was adopted unanimously. Not even Rourke made much of a peep.

"Thank you," Dr. Jay told the council. "I hope we can all get together and do something for the city."

It was the calm before the storm.

The feds, state, and county had approved our application for funds for the new central fire station and emergency operating center. The firehouse was as old as our public schools, built just after the Civil War. It was a two-story brick building designed for fire engines pulled by horses, not modern trucks. It had few sanitary facilities and a gaping hole in the second floor. The firemen's beds were supported by four concrete blocks instead of proper bedposts. Albany County wanted us to build a new fire house, as did Cohoesiers. It was Cohoesier Democrat Alderwoman Emma Shea who flared up over it.

The plan and specifications were ready to be bid out. All we needed now was a $190,000 bond issue for the city's share of the cost, and we could build the new fire house. During a special hearing, Bob Curran introduced an ordinance for the full amount of the bond issue. It was snowing pretty hard that night, but the place was packed; 400 people had stayed for the meeting's full four hours.

The press described it as one of the wildest and most uncontrolled meetings in recent years, with Dawson constantly interrupting the speakers and refusing to sit down. The police tried to approach him, but Dawson's followers and wife blocked their path, creating a blockade around him. Eventually, every time he'd interrupt, the crowd would roar back at him.

It had all started getting out of hand when the four Democratic aldermen, led by Emma Shea, stated that they of course supported the fire house but not our means of getting it. Alderman Shea demanded to know why she was left out of the negotiations and had not been shown the plans. We didn't know what she was talking about. There hadn't been any negotiations, and the Democratic aldermen all knew we had applied for funds for plans that were made publicly available.

"It's not my job to educate you about your job. The plans were on display in City Hall at the engineer's office. They were open to the public," Bob Curran told her. "Not one of you Democrat aldermen asked to see them," he said.

Dawson piped up, "I looked at them, and I have investigated the site on Central Ave., and I find the whole thing too costly."

Dr. Jay told him to sit down. Then Dawson claimed to have talked with Congressman O'Brien, an O'Connell-backed guy, who told him that the funds were not secure.

The Mayor showed the crowd a telegram from Congressman O'Brien. The telegram assured us that the federal funds were secure. "I wish you and the City of Cohoes well on its new fire house," Rep. O'Brien signed off.

When I wrote the application for the grant, I worked with two-time Olympic gold medalist sprinter and Bronze Star recipient for his bomber service in WWII Ray Barbuti. Ray was now the state's deputy director of emergency management, also known then as the state's civil defense. Ray told me that we didn't need to worry about getting Albany County approval for the firehouse because "Rocky," the Governor, "owed us one" for vetoing our bill on elected school board referendums. Ray turned out to be right.

I also had received a handwritten letter from Congressman O'Brien after our election offering his support.

Dawson didn't understand that losers in an election become orphans. Although he had tried to make the night about him, Fire Chief Grogan had the final word. "How anyone can oppose this project is beyond reason. Our living conditions are unbearable, yet our men are forced to spend one third of their lives under these conditions. We ask for unanimous approval."

At the next council meeting the bond issue was approved. The following August, construction began on the new central fire station and emergency operating center. In November, Fire Chief Grogan died. The fire station was subsequently named for him.

CHAPTER TWENTY-EIGHT

OUR WAR ON POVERTY

For the rest of our term, that is how it went: democrats engaged in a cynical game of rule or ruin, while we used grants, innovation, collaboration, and vision to accomplish what we had promised.

The urban blight that had plagued downtown Cohoes was one of our main focuses, in part because I was confident that I could use my civil engineering background to help write successful grant applications. President Johnson's War on Poverty was designed precisely for towns and cities like Cohoes. In February 1965, we learned that our application to fund a "Neighborhood Youth Corps" had been approved by the federal government. It would be a training program for eighty-eight high school dropouts or potential dropouts between the ages of sixteen and twenty-one. Ours was the first in the state and one of only seventeen nationally. We hired a highly qualified candidate to direct the program, Larry Favreau.

Soon afterward, we learned we'd received funding for a low-income family child development center for preschoolers, to provide them with social and pre-academic skills, as well as a good breakfast and lunch. I had written the grant to include the YWCA as the program sponsor. It took only three weeks to get up and running once we'd received the funds, and it quickly filled to capacity. Word of our success got around, and later that year, Albany Junior College chose our child development center as the training ground for nursery school teachers.

By the time we had the children's program operating, we learned that our senior citizens center had also been awarded a federal grant. For that program, I had designated the local Catholic charities organization as the sponsor. It was spearheaded by two young progressive priests.

The accolades kept coming. That spring, we received a letter from Sargent Shriver, head of the Federal Economic Opportunity Commission and President Kennedy's brother-in-law. In the letter, he praised our projects, noting that we were viewed as the pioneers of Johnson's War on Poverty. I was invited to a state conference to discuss our practical application of the anti-poverty ethos of the Economic Opportunity Act.

That summer, Virginia, Cohoes's first lady, started a fundraising campaign to construct a community center. Meanwhile, Larry Favreau announced that in its first seven months of operation, the Neighborhood Youth Corps had a hundred enrollees, and best of all, already a quarter of the enrollees had secured permanent jobs. This success helped us secure funding for a second year.

As the mayor's representative, I coordinated with the Economic Opportunity and the Recreation Commissions to apply for federal funds to improve our citywide swimming pool at Lansing Park. Our plan was to construct separate male and female restrooms and shower facilities, a food service area, a first aid station, and a maintenance area. The project was funded. In August, the Common Council approved a $172,525 park improvement program with matching federal funds for outdoor recreation facilities for six city parks.

One of the objectives of our local anti-poverty campaign was the rehabilitation of substandard housing. According to our comprehensive plan, out of 6,241 housing units in Cohoes, 1,741 were deteriorating and 1,697 were too dilapidated to reclaim. To help us address this depression in housing stock, we applied to receive state funds for a Housing, Environmental, Research and Development Center, which we received. Additionally, the state approved further funding for two hometown beautification projects.

In November, Virginia announced that the Cohoes Community Center Building Fund Campaign intended to raise $333,500 to be matched by federal dollars. Our new firehouse was due to be completed in December. Rounding out the year was the announcement from the school board that by January 1968, the new high school would be set to open its doors.

A personal milestone for me came when the American Society for Public Administration awarded me the Governor Charles Evans Hughes Award "for courageous, resourceful and imaginative work in reorganizing the government and contributing to the future development of the city of Cohoes." Normally given to a state official, it was the first time the award went to a local government official.

CHAPTER TWENTY-NINE

TURK'S DEMISE

As a group, we had largely gained the trust of voters. But within our group, the power players were scheming, and Turk was getting sloppy. Until being named public works director, Turk's employment track record pretty much amounted to standing in line for his unemployment insurance or being let go from one part-time job after another. Once, I got him a job as a laborer on the interstate, but he never made the effort to move up the ranks. What could have been a career opportunity with a little work ethic became a dead-end instead.

When we won the election, I kept remembering the steaks and butter he was known to steal. The more successes we racked up with our progressive programs, and seeing how they truly helped people, the more uneasy I felt with his opportunistic ways.

Thinking back to a time when we were in elementary school, Turk said to me, "You get in my wagon and stand up, and I'll pull you around the block." I did what he told me to do, but he pulled the wagon so hard and fast out from under me that I hit the pavement and got a concussion.

In May 1965, Turk attended a statewide public works conference in Syracuse. On the last day of the conference, Harold Zwinge, head mechanic for the Public Works Department and Turk's brother-in-law, drove the city of Cohoes's grader machine ten miles out of town to the construction site of a new school in Brittonskill. The grader was left there for the better part of a week. During that time, it was used by the private construction firm belonging to one of Turk's in-laws. Joe Garrett, our commissioner of public safety got an anonymous tip about it. So Joe drove up to Brittonskill, snapped a few pictures, and wrote up a report for the mayor. The following day, the grader reappeared in Cohoes.

Joe kept digging into Turk's activities. He discovered that Turk was paying his water inspector, Harold Jurgens, overtime. The problem was that Jurgens was on vacation in Florida.

Paul Coughlin wrote up formal charges against Turk, since he was entitled to a hearing before the mayor. Testimony would be heard under oath. Coughlin represented the city, and Willard Frament represented Senecal. There was a lot of conflicting testimony. Senecal gave three different cover stories regarding the grader.

Coughlin discredited each of Turk's alibis and got him to admit under oath that he had made false statements. Meanwhile, Carl Engstrom, as deputy corporation counsel, testified on behalf of Turk that he had discussed Jurgens's overtime pay with Senecal, Rourke, and Curran, which Curran denied.

Curran was always a bit preachy, but I still had a lot of respect for him. He really was a reformer, so when Engstrom lumped him in with Senecal and Rourke, implicating him in a lie, any goodwill Bob might have had toward Senecal evaporated. Bob was fairly rabid about it and called Senecal every name in the book after that.

As mayor, Dr. Jay had to listen to all of this nonsense, which was hard for him, since some of the Senecal family were his patients. The evidence against Turk was compelling, and Dr. Jay ruled that Turk had to be dismissed from his post. Turk appealed the decision to the State Supreme Court and lost. He went to the appellate division and lost that one, too.

The battle hadn't ended in the courts, though. Despite having a fulltime job, Rourke somehow found time to attend every one of Turk's hearings. He coached witnesses from the aisles, nodding yes or no to the questions being asked, until Dr. Jay admonished his behavior.

After that, Rourke distributed a flier with the Citizens Party banner across it, proclaiming Senecal's innocence. That was a bridge too far for Bob Curran. Bob called a meeting of the leadership members of the Citizens Party. They voted Rourke out.

At the next council meeting, Rourke introduced an ordinance to form a committee "to conduct a full and complete public investigation...into any and all matters concerning the operation of each and every office." The Democrats voted in a bloc to approve the committee. There was no specific allegation, however, so Stanton Ablett ruled on it and advised the mayor to veto it. The only way to reverse a mayoral veto would have been if five out of the six aldermen voted to do so. Rourke did not have the votes. His witch hunt ended before it began.

CHAPTER THIRTY

DAWSON IS NEXT: 1964-1967

Not long after we took office in 1964, Sam Quimet, a local real estate and insurance agent, volunteered his time to work with the assessors in reassessing properties. A local rag called the *Newsweekly* ran an article claiming Sam was scamming the city. Another article said that I had stuffed a jacket into a sewer in Manor Heights to clog it up and make the Santspree administration look bad. The paper published several such libelous stories about Citizens Party Leaders.

Sam sued the paper for libel and slander. Meanwhile, I wanted to know who owned the paper, so I brought criminal charges for violations of a state law requiring the names of all publishers of the newspaper to be listed publicly.

A jury trial uncovered the paper's publishers: Bill Dawson and the Cohoes City Democratic Committee were its principal owners. They were found guilty of hiding their identity and fined several thousand dollars. The Internal Revenue Service took notice and brought liens against the *Newsweekly* owners for failure to withhold and pay taxes. Poor Sam did not get any money for damages, since after paying the fines, the paper went out of business. But that was not to be the end of the matter.

Earlier that year, in an article published by his employer, *The Troy Record*, Dawson was quoted saying that he and his people would fight long and hard to regain power. He boasted he would win back the two assessor and three supervisor seats he'd lost, saying the Citizens Party supervisors "just make a lot of noise."

Soon after, the Democratic supervisor from the First Ward died, and the Council voted 4 to 3 to appoint a Citizen to fill the unexpired term. That brought the total number of Citizens occupying county supervisor seats to four, a setback for Dawson.

What really stopped his roll through the Citizens' ascendancy, however, was losing his chairmanship of the Democratic committee. That happened over the next summer in 1966, after a federal grand jury indictment for personal income tax evasion.

Federal agents approached me to ask what I could tell them about Dawson. I knew what everyone else knew. He was an editorial cartoonist for a local paper who somehow could afford to drive a big black Lincoln Continental. His wife shopped at expensive stores. And, of course, there was the swimming pool in their backyard. I also knew that even though he was not a city employee and technically had no jurisdiction over city affairs, anyone doing business with the city had to pay Dawson a "tribute" before they could get paid for their services.

I told the guy from the IRS, "I got a couple of affidavits about his using city money to build his pool, if you want them." He wanted them.

I wasn't really the informant. It was Red Smith, the son of Warren Smith, who filled that role. Given that politics was the family business, Red was also a Democrat, but he didn't see eye to eye with Dawson. He had made a play for the Democratic committee chairmanship in 1964 and lost to Dawson, creating bad blood between them. Red offered the IRS enough evidence to indict Dawson with a federal grand jury.

At Dawson's federal trial that summer in 1967, Dawson's wife greeted people at the courthouse doors like it was a party and she was the hostess. One of the feds' witnesses, a housing developer, testified that he gave Dawson $1,750 in cash. Shortly afterward, the city installed water and sewer facilities at one of his developments.

Dawson actually testified under oath that his word was the law in Cohoes but denied taking any kickbacks. Any money given to him at the Elks Club were tributes and party donations, he claimed. When the party records were presented to the court, there was a stir: Dawson had been keeping them in Japanese.

"Do you or anyone of the committeemen speak Japanese?" the judge asked.

Dawson said he had learned it while serving as an interpreter in WWII. Then Dawson claimed that the money hadn't come from city vendors at all, but from his great uncle, Mike Smith. He hadn't been able to claim it because he didn't know how much there was; it had been kept in a tin under his aunt's bed for years, and he hadn't been able to access it.

He was found guilty of not reporting nearly $50,000 in income for 1959 and 1961 and sentenced to two years in federal penitentiary. He remained free on a $2,500 bail bond while his case was appealed, but ultimately, he served his time until he got early parole.

Years later, Dawson called me up and wanted to know if I would meet with him. "Sure, I'll meet with you," I told him. That was nearly twenty years ago. I had left Cohoes a long time before that.

He was in a wheelchair. He had a lot of land, he told me. He wanted to build an assisted living project on it and asked me what kind of federal programs were available. He asked if I could help him with the grant applications. Our conversation was short. I knew he'd purchased the land illegally during the Santspree administration. The council had passed an ordinance to let him purchase land for back taxes, all without a public auction. There wasn't much I could advise him about.

He wanted to discuss what was going on in Russia for some reason. Then suddenly he said, "I don't have any animosity toward you. You beat me fair and square. It's that Red Smith, that's the son of a bitch that turned me into the IRS."

A few years later, Dawson died. I happened to be in Cohoes at the time, so I attended his wake. Mrs. Dawson was very pleasant and thanked me for coming. That was that. I suppose time really can heal all wounds.

CHAPTER THIRTY-ONE

SEWERS, CANALS, AND ELECTIONS: 1965

Dawson's indictment came just before the 1965 midterm elections. He was diminished but not silenced, and from the sidelines, he chimed in with Willard Frament to accuse the Citizens Party of being nothing more than tax-raising noisemakers run by a political boss—me.

Ignoring that, I stuck with the playbook from our 1963 campaign, this time hammering home how many of our promises had turned into actual accomplishments. I knew this was going to be a difficult election despite our progress. The midterm elections did not have the same energy and enthusiasm as the citywide elections. Our workers from the 1963 campaign were worn out and needed motivation. For the Machine workers, running an election was a conditioned reflex. Once again, we needed those people who voted in the presidential and gubernatorial election but not the local. It was a difficult enough task to get them to vote in the citywide election, but it was nearly impossible in the midterm election. Plus, now that the Machine had our turncoat, Frank Rourke, four of the six aldermen, and three of the six county supervisors; assessors were split evenly along party lines.

Turk Senecal ran on the Republican ticket against our candidate, Ralph Robinson, for county supervisor in the Fifth Ward. Naturally, Frank Rourke was his Campaign Manager. The Republicans and Democrats ganged up on us, filing petitions for an independent line on the voting machines. This probably would have confused a significant number of voters who wanted to support our independent ticket. Fortunately (and predictably), their petitions were so incoherent that the Board of Elections threw them out.

Our campaign focused on what to do with the fetid sewers and canals. During the election, *The Troy Record* ran an article about the dangers posed by the canals, showing a picture of two young boys sitting on the wall of a canal with their feet in the water. Aside from the filth, there was the risk of drowning.

Our administration had purchased the canals and planned to build a park and playground. Whether it was strategic maneuvering or fear based on a fundamental inability to understand basic concepts of civil engineering, the Democrats would not accept that it was to everyone's benefit that we take over the canals and fill them in.

To start, we needed those canals to address compliance with federal and state mandates that we intercept sewage and treat it before discharging it into the Mohawk and Hudson Rivers. Cesspools had been roiling in the rivers for years, with Troy, Albany, and Schenectady also dumping sewage straight into the Hudson. All of the developments along those canals were dumping their sewage in the canals—residential and commercial. We also needed the canal to tie in all the sewer lines into an intercept. After that, we could fill it, eliminate what had become a known drowning risk and develop it into a green space as an added benefit to the community. The alternative would have been to construct new routes off the canals, which would be expensive and time-consuming.

If Alderman Emma Shea, whose district the canal was in, had read the city charter, she would have seen that the Board of Estimate and Apportionment had the authority to acquire land on request from the public works commissioner, which is what had happened, and all for the tidy sum of $1. It wasn't a secret.

During a council meeting that fall, Alderman Shea and her fellow Democrats objected to the plan and suggested that the mayor demand that Niagara Mohawk stop maintaining a "public nuisance" and give them sixty days to fill in the canals. Then, if the power company refused, the mayor could have the city do it and send Niagara Mohawk the bill. In any case, the mayor was not about to antagonize Niagara Mohawk. They contributed the water to the canals, while Cohoesiers contributed the sewage.

"I ask you, who is responsible for the canal being a nuisance?" The mayor retorted to Emma. "If Niagara Mohawk filled the canals in completely, it would block all sewage, which would back up into everyone's homes and flood the streets."

When Bob Curran introduced an ordinance for a bond issue of $80,000 to cover the sewer intercept and the associated costs of filling the No. 2 and No. 3 canals, bedlam erupted. The Democrats on the council accused the mayor of taking on an enormous liability and of not knowing "the length of tunnels and the depths which they go."

But we did know because we'd had them assessed by the power company. Moreover, with thirteen children already drowned in the canals, we knew the liability was far greater if we didn't fill them in. The discord led to Curran tabling the ordinance until a public hearing on the bond could be held.

Rourke and the three other council Democrats voted to delay the project, which meant that even though they had effectively stopped the project in its tracks, they could say later on that they had not voted against it.

Dr. Jay called out their game, saying it was, "political treachery at its worst," since they knew full well that their constituents wanted the canals filled in. In fact, the Machine was handing us a golden opportunity to expose its usual rank ignorance.

A few days later, the mayor and I joined other members of the administration and the Council President, Bob Curran, for a Paris sewer-style adventure. Wearing hip boots and carrying flashlights, walkie talkies, and a camera, we descended into the Ontario Street tunnel, constructed in 1830, which connected the open canals. We proceeded through the seventeen-foot-wide tunnel by boat. There was neither a brick nor stone out of place, and the mortar was solid. There was no reason they wouldn't last another hundred years or more.

It was bedlam again on the night we gave a public presentation of our sewer tour and tunnel inspection. Emma Shea turned up the volume on her outrage and accused Dr. Jay of breaking the law by purchasing the canals. When she declared him "unfit for office," she brought on a chorus of boos that quickly became cheers when Dr. Jay reminded her that just the night before in a television news interview, Emma had said, "No one questions the mayor's integrity."

A young boy in the audience walked up to the mayor and gave him a dollar. He told Dr. Jay he wanted to see him start the project, and someone else called out, "You cannot put a dollar sign on human life, and I would gladly spend $80,000 to save one kid "

Emma Shea, grasping for any way to discredit Dr. Jay, demanded proof that the city had purchased the canals. Her fellow Democrat, Alderman Skawinski, accused Jay of using the canals as "a political plum just before election."

In fact, the Citizens did win four of the six supervisor seats, giving us one more seat than before. We also won both assessor seats.

Even though *The Troy Record* said it was a vote of confidence for our first two years in office, I read it this way: even with Dawson gone, the Democrats were still strong and could win with good candidates and active campaigning. The Republicans less so, but they remained a factor.

The Democrats had come within striking distance. I was concerned that even with all of our progress, the 1967 citywide election was going to be a tough one. I was worried. There were 800 voters—Citizens supporters—who'd sat out this election. If they had participated this time around, we could have taken all six wards.

CHAPTER THIRTY-TWO

THE INS AND OUTS OF JUSTICE: POLITICS AND THE COURTS: 1966

We didn't have much time to savor our victory before we were engaged in a multi-front battle. The first skirmish was the budget. During the previous summer, the state legislature enacted a statewide sales tax, which meant all cities had to reinstate their 3% utility tax. In Cohoes, this equaled about $50,000.

We also needed money to pay the principal and interest on bonds issued by the previous administration and to maintain our recreation budget and War on Poverty programs.

Of course, Aldermen Rourke and Shea objected to the utility tax, saying funds from a recent state sales tax levy would cover the difference. Bob Curran reminded the two Democrats that they had voted for the 1965 budget, which had included the utility tax as revenue, before voting to drop the tax.

We now had deep concerns about our 1966 budget. The Democrats had a majority on the Common Council, and Rourke was their ad hoc leader. The question was whether they would support our programs or continue to obstruct progress.

The city charter called for the Board of Estimate and Apportionment to prepare the annual budget estimate and submit it to the Common Council for approval. The charter stipulated that the council could neither touch salaries or debt payments nor increase line items; however, it did have the power to reduce them.

The Democrats began their assault on our city improvement plans by tabling an ordinance for a bond issue to improve the water system. Then, during the budget hearing that February, they ignored the budget from the Board of Estimate and Apportionment. Instead, Rourke introduced a resolution of his own. He specifically designed his budget to disrupt our ability to run the city's day-to-day business, never mind carry out our promised improvement programs. He called for a 14% decrease in the tax rate, cuts to snow removal funds, restrictions on the purchase and maintenance of equipment, materials, supplies, utilities, and other critical operational costs. They also cut the funds specifically for Paul Coughlin: Turk's vendetta, thinly disguised.

The budget hearing played to a full house. Rourke's budget was met by boos and shouts of "You are turning back the clock!" Our corporation counsel, Stanton Ablett, called Rourke's bluff: the city charter stated that the budget had to be introduced as an ordinance, not a resolution. It's not possible to veto a resolution. What do you do with a resolution? It's not much more than an expression of intent.

At the next meeting, Rourke came prepared with his budget presented as an ordinance. The Democrats voted in favor of Rourke's budget as a bloc, but Dr. Jay vetoed it. Rourke couldn't get the votes to overturn the veto, so we were left without a budget. If the council couldn't pass a budget, then the issue would go to court. The court would be obligated to rule in favor of adopting the Board of Estimate and Apportionment's budget—the one sanctioned by Dr. Jay.

When I told Coughlin all this, he replied, "So, what we have to do is get one of the city-chartered department heads to sue the Common Council to adopt the board's budget."

We had Tom Donnelly, the city comptroller, sue the Common Council in the State Supreme Court for failure to adopt a budget in the required thirty-day window. The suit cited, among several items, that the pressure was on the city to meet a bond payment by April 1 or face default. Paul Coughlin represented Donnelly. The council had agreed to put in escrow the difference between the budget from City Hall and Rourke's budget, pending the court's decision. Throughout the fight, played out routinely in the press, local merchants voiced support for Dr. Jay and demanded his budget be adopted.

Carl Engstrom represented the Democrats. This did not surprise me; I knew he was going to turn on us when we brought Turk up on charges. Without Turk, Carl had no leverage.

We won. Rourke and the three Democrats on the council appealed to the Appellate Division of the State's Court of Appeals. In a unanimous decision, we won again. The Dems appealed again, this time to the State Court of Appeals. About three months passed with no word on the progress of the suit.

Coughlin wondered what was taking so long to get the final decision, so he asked me to go see my Uncle Walter, who was good friends with the chief justice of the Court of Appeals.

"We don't want him to rule one way or the other; we just want them to rule!" Coughlin told me.

The truth was that Walter Wertime had started to pay more attention to me since we'd overturned the Machine. Defeating them was something he hadn't been able to do, even though he had wanted to. He helped to get things moving, and we finally got the decision: with two of O'Connell's guys on the bench, it wasn't a unanimous decision, but it was in our favor.

Rourke went berserk. He couldn't figure out how, with a 4 to 2 council vote, he couldn't win and pass his own budget. Years later, he told me, "I don't know how the hell you could do that."

Now we had our budget. Our victory had garnered the attention of nearly sixty mayors statewide, including John Lindsay of

New York City, who sent a telegram expressing his support for Dr. Jay and our administration.

Once the budget was in place, questions arose about the deputy counsel, Carl Engstrom, regarding why he'd testified on behalf of Turk, who had appeared to be profiting from under-the-table deals using city property. Stanton Ablett asked for Engstrom's resignation, and Engstrom conceded.

Meanwhile, the continual harassment by the Democratic faction of the council landed us once again in the State Supreme Court. This time, Emma Shea and her sister filed a taxpayer suit to show cause for the acquisition of the power canals. They claimed it should be null and void because the Common Council did not approve of the acquisition. However, the city charter stated clearly that the commissioner of public works has the power to acquire land with the approval of the Board of Estimate and Apportionment (not the Common Council). The Sheas' attorney managed to get the case in front of a Supreme Court Judge appointed by Dan O'Connell. The judge ruled in their favor, which meant we had to go back to the State Appellate Court.

Our hopes were high. At the time the Shea's were suing us, Stanley Van Rensselear, our state assemblyman, drafted a bill to have the state fill in the Champlain Canal if Cohoes installed a sewer intercept. To our surprise, Senator Julian Erway, a Democrat, said he would introduce it in the Senate. All that the bill needed was for the Cohoes Common Council to pass a resolution in support of it. Emma Shea said she needed additional information and copies of agreements between the parties. The resolution passed, but Senator Erway submitted the bill too late for Senate approval.

Meanwhile, two more cars flipped into the canals. There were no casualties, but the accidents focused attention on the dangers the canals posed. I dove into action. The canal in Emma Shea's First Ward stunk. Mattresses and heaps of other debris floated on stagnant brown water. I posted a sign along the bank of the canal: "The reason your playground isn't being built is because Alderman Emma Shea and her sister brought an injunction against the McDonald administration to cease all work toward acquiring the canals from Niagara Mohawk Power Company and filling in the canals and building a public park."

Emma went nuts when she saw that. Her niece was Paul Coughlin's wife, Frannie. Now Frannie was blasting Paul to make me get rid of that sign.

He came to me and said, "Come on, Paul, can you take that sign down?"

"Sure, I'll take it down, Paul."

In another week, he said, "Paul, did you do it?"

"No, jeez, I forgot. I'll take it down. Don't worry about it." Days later, I took it down, but the damage was done.

It took about a year, but we won on appeal, and Emma's neighborhood got its beautiful park with a playground, all built with federal funds and support from the power company.

CHAPTER THIRTY-THREE

ALL-AMERICA CITY

On October 16, 1966, the headline on the front page of *The Troy Record* read, "Cohoes Finalist in All-America Cities Test." Given by the National Municipal League and *Look Magazine*, the award, considered the "Nobel Prize" for constructive citizenship, recognized and celebrated communities using best practices in community engagement to address critical civic issues. It was a moment of celebration, but one of gravity, too. Despite the Democrats' heated attempts to draw the Citizens back from success, in just thirty-three months, we had taken a city, choked as it was in the corrupt grip of a decades-old political machine, and had resurrected it. The effect of our transparency and optimism was so comprehensive, so transformational; we were considered exemplary on a national platform. We were being honored for what can be done when people cooperate and govern according to the rule of law. Specifically citing our citizen participation, the National Municipal League and *Look Magazine* designated Cohoes to compete against twenty-one other municipalities for the top prize for the communities that best exemplified the American spirit of governance at a local level.

In November, representatives from each of the finalists were to appear in Boston before a twelve-person jury headed by Dr. George H. Gallup to present their case for why their city should be chosen. Finalists had ten minutes each, followed by five minutes of questions from the jury. The winner would be announced the following spring.

Dr. Jay asked Paul Coughlin and me to argue the case for Cohoes and stated publicly, "I consider this a fine tribute to all the people of the community. All the people in Cohoes should be proud of themselves."

The Democrats back home were quoted in the papers saying, "We always knew Cohoes was an All-America City."

A citizen delegation was created, and on the day of our presentation before the All-America Jury, chartered buses with more than 200 Cohoesiers set out for Boston. A crowd of Cohoesiers assembled, with many crying with tears of joy and pride. The Keveny Band played as they waved their neighbors and loved ones off to represent our town. Our delegation brought signs and buttons to hand out at an exhibit hall. The presentations to the jury were made in the late afternoon and were followed by a Cohoes-sponsored cocktail reception. For many Cohoesiers, this was an unfathomable, once-in-a-lifetime moment.

After the buses arrived, our people were milling in the hotel lobby. Our City Hall janitor, Mike, one of the delegates, was standing like a sentinel adjacent to the bar room door. He flagged me down.

"Don't go in that bar," he told me.

I asked, "Why? What is the problem?"

"I asked for a bottle of beer, put down my dollar bill, and they did not give me any change," Mike said. He was used to thirty-five cent beers back home. Being in the big city where beers were a buck, he thought the city slickers were taking advantage of us.

When Paul Coughlin started his speech, his voice was cracking from the pressure and emotion, but it was still clear. He started with a quote from Chief Justice Oliver Wendell Homes, "It is required of a man that he should share the passion and action of his time at peril of being judged not to have lived." Paul used his time to narrate how the history of our city's corrupt political machine had led to the formation of the Citizens Party and our triumph of 1963. He described the kinds of intimidation and kickbacks that had helped Dawson rule the city, drawing a good laugh from the jury when he told them, "The last political dictator of Cohoes stated this past summer during his federal income tax trial, where he was found guilty, that 'my word was law.'"

When it was my turn to speak, my knees were wobbling uncontrollably, but my voice was loud and clear. I outlined the many promises we had kept, and our other achievements accomplished under Dr. Jay's leadership. We both emphasized the extent of citizen participation in these triumphs and emphasized that we were good people acting out of common sense rather than dogma. We described how we mobilized our citizenry and businesses to successfully participate in our government and its programs. I finished my speech one second before the bell rang saying, "Today the people of Cohoes can be judged."

When we'd finished, delegates and supporters from Cohoes, decorated with flowers and buttons on their lapels, stood and applauded. Several members of the jury did, too.

With a prescience I did not recognize at the time, Dr. Gallup asked me what would prevent the Citizens from eventually becoming guilty of the kinds of corruption we'd overthrown. Somewhat emotional and with so many of my fellow Cohoesiers literally standing behind me, I explained that now that we'd come out from under the pall of dictatorship, our attitudes were informed by freedom, and we would continue to operate within the law, with each citizen keeping the others in check. When our revolution arose, the citizens rose with it.

We had brought Dr. Joe Perrotta, our new superintendent of schools, with us, in case the jury had any questions. One member of the jury, who was the head of the National Education Association, asked about the reforms in our school district. Perrotta reeled off a dozen recent improvements. Joe was impressive; it had been a good strategy to bring him.

We rented the Hampton Room for a party after our presentation. There was an open bar for our delegates, and we invited the Pinellas County group to join us. Cohoesiers love a party. The room was full of energy, gaiety, and goodwill.

The only snafu of the night occurred because the bartender had mixed up a batch of martinis in a metal pitcher. Later, when a new bartender came on shift, he mistook a martini pitcher for water and used it to pour orders of Scotch and water. We had to carry a few of our delegates off to bed.

We would not know the jury's verdict for another three months.

CHAPTER THIRTY-FOUR

ACTS OF DECENCY: 1967

As was now customary, the presentation of the 1967 annual budget evoked grandstanding and high drama. Dr. Jay announced that for 1967, we were already running a $53,000 surplus for the third consecutive year. It felt like a Broadway show, an annual spectacle for Cohoesiers to see their government in action.

Dawson, still out on bail, appeared at the meeting and declared our numbers a hoax. "It's not a hoax," Dr. Jay said. "And that surplus even includes your having paid your $43,411 fine," he added, referring to the penalty Dawson paid for his misconduct as a secret publisher of the local propaganda paper.

Rourke positioned himself as the leader of the opposition, and with the three Democrats egging him on, challenged every single line item until the meeting ended well after 1:00 a.m. It was all for show. Everyone knew that Rourke's attempts to derail the mayor's budget were pure follies. The state's Court of Appeals had already made clear that if council failed to pass a budget, then the one presented by the Board of Estimate and Apportionment would be adopted.

This meant that all twenty-five department heads who attended the hearing were subjected to Rourke's sanctimony as he questioned their tallies. Ultimately, Rourke was forced to concede that the budget was fairly solid. The budget passed.

During this time, encouraged by the All-America City experience, I prepared an application for a federal grant under the Model Cities Program, a demonstration project to see what worked to reverse urban decay. After I completed the application, we got the news we'd all been waiting for: we had been chosen "An All-America City." Telegrams of congratulations flooded in from U.S. Senators Robert F. Kennedy and Jacob Javits, Governor Rockefeller, and even First Lady Johnson. Vice President Hubert Humphrey and Sargent Shriver also congratulated us.

It was all hands on deck to put together the necessary celebrations. It took over a month to plan. We had a mammoth parade with eleven divisions, each with a marching band and numerous floats. Dr. Jay was the parade's grand marshal. Paul Coughlin and I acted as deputy marshals, followed by thirty-two honorary marshals on palomino horseback. More than 38,000 people attended the three-hour spectacle from all over the capital district.

At the reviewing stands, Richard Childs, Chairman of the National Municipal League, presented Dr. Jay with the All-America City Award. David Maxey, *Look Magazine's* editor, presented Dr. Jay with the All-America City Flag, stating that he was presenting it to "an aroused citizenry who will commit decency for their own good." Later that evening, during a victory celebration at the state armory, U.S. Representative Dan Button gave the keynote address. Maxey stated that becoming an All-America City was not a destiny, but a journey requiring sustained progress and effort.

Over 400 people attended the banquet and ball. The New York Times ran a front-page article in its Sunday upstate section, including several pictures of our parade. We concluded with a fireworks show that attracted more than 4,000 people to Lansing Park.

Still, I knew that with a citywide election coming up, we could not rest on our laurels.

The new central fire station and emergency operation center (circa 1966), built with federal, state and local funds, replaced the old central station built in 1867. The emergency operating center was below ground and housed the dormitories, communication center, fuel and food for one month, kitchen and medical clinic. Dawson led the opposition to the project. (Photo by Jim Shaughnessy).

The Cohoes Community Center was one of the high profile promises of our 1963 campaign. Dr. Jay's wife, Virginia led a community fund raising and raised $400,000 and then I wrote a successful application for federal funds for $600,000 to construct the center. The Community Center has served all ages for recreational and social services for nearly 50 years.

As part of our administrative reforms, Cohoes' was the first city in the capital district to implement a data processing center (circa 1967) producing our assessment roll, city and county tax billings, utility billings and accounting. (Photo by Jim Shaughnessy).

Cohoes' "All-America City Parade" on April 8, 1967. In just over 3 years the Citizen Party brought Cohoes from the dominance of a corrupt political machine to national recognition, being selected as an All-America city. This picture shows the reviewing stand in front of city hall with public and community leaders viewing our three hour parade. The New York Times wrote, "...would not have looked thin on Fifth Avenue." (Photo by William T. Riley)

CHAPTER THIRTY-FIVE

ACTS OF HARM

Maybe the momentum of our success was too much for those who had tried to stop it in its tracks. Maybe certain factions were envious of the accolades and recognition that the Citizens Party was receiving.

One Sunday that summer in 1967, I was driving with my four-year-old son on one of the many Cohoes back roads. I wasn't in any hurry, which was a good thing, as it turned out. All of a sudden, we saw a car wheel bouncing its way through a farmer's field. We looked at it, wondering where it came from. Then, the car started wobbling. I knew then, that's my car's wheel bouncing away, the axel broke. I tried to put on the brake; it was also gone. I figured out the only way I could stop the car was to use the gravel shoulder. I hoped the friction from the gravel would be enough to slow me down. I was surprised to find that a car could still run on three wheels. Once we came to a stop, I went over to the farmer's yard to retrieve my tire. The farmer came out to see what was happening, and I asked if I could use his phone. I called a tow truck, and we made it back to town. We never did make it to K-Mart.

The next day, I went to see my car.

"Here I want to show you this," Ray said. "This thing has been cut." He had a confused expression on his face.

It looked like a hacksaw had cut halfway through the axel on the circumference.

You could see the fresh break where it came apart. I admit, I had felt some fear. Dawson was delusional and imperious, but he wasn't a murderer. But somebody had deliberately vandalized my car, hoping that my wheel would fly off. I remembered what Kellogg had told me once about Rourke wanting to burn me up in a pool of gasoline. As far as I knew, Rourke was the only person to threaten my life.

"You want me to call the police?" Ray asked me, "Paul...?"

"No, no, no. No." I came back to the moment. I didn't want the police getting involved. First, whoever it was, I didn't want that person to know the scheme had nearly succeeded. Second, if the police got involved, then so would the press. I didn't want to dissuade people from participating in local government or voicing opposition due to fear of retribution. It was like before when our tax assessments had been raised. We didn't tell anyone since it had been so hard to get people to overcome their fears of the Machine.

From that moment on, though, "I watched my every step."

CHAPTER THIRTY-SIX

ELECTION TURMOIL: 1967

About a month after the hacksaw incident, it was election season again. I saw it as a referendum on our commitments made and kept. We had been in and out of court ten times since 1963, more than any other city in the state. The opposition seemed determined to obstruct our progress at every turn, but we had demonstrated time and again we were willing to fight for what we believed in, including the next election. I was again Campaign Manager for the Citizens Party and decided that if it ain't broke, don't fix it. We would replicate our strategies of old. We sponsored rallies and parades to drum up support.

I wanted to focus our campaign on our achievements and awards since we had gained office: the All-America City award, the canal conversions that gave the city six new or rebuilt parks and playgrounds, and a track record of successful projects and programs endorsed by broad citizen participation. We had put in place a civil service system based on merit and given city employees pay raises, health insurance, and retirement benefits. Their support alone could help us overcome the voter gap we would need to take us across the finish line.

In the 1965 election, we'd only taken 52% of the vote citywide and only narrowly won the assessor seats. In that election, we had only 9,519 registered voters. Now, we needed their votes, plus an additional 800. My strategy was to send out a letter to all city employees, outlining the benefits they'd enjoyed under our stewardship. Those employees and their families probably accounted for 1,000 votes.

We conducted our usual poll-watching training and canvassed our voters for registration. Approximately 10,500 voters registered. We'd motivated most of the people who generally only voted for president and governor to register for the election. These were the non-Machine voters who would support us on Election Day.

Rourke was the ad hoc Campaign Manager for the Democratic Party. He emulated our 1963 campaign model, but he also chose to run smear campaigns against the Citizens Party and ad hominem attacks on me. The career politicians also wanted us out. The Republicans and Democrats were cross-endorsing candidates, ganging up on us by working together. The Democrats had put candidates on at least three rows on the voting machines (Democrat, Conservative, and Liberal), while we had only one.

In addition to our incumbents, we added Ernie Hatch in the Third Ward, Eben Patrick in the First, and Eddie Rusecki for county supervisor. The Democrats were running John Marra, Harry's brother, for Mayor. John was an undertaker and the Albany County coroner, a seat he'd won by a large margin with help from Dan O'Connell. This brought in the Albany County organization. O'Connell liked Marra more than he ever did Dawson, and Rourke was delighted to be in with the Machine. He'd even approached some Citizens offering to be a power broker between us and O'Connell's people. We told Rourke we'd be sure people knew he was in with the Machine now.

As before, our campaign focused on what we'd promised, and what we'd delivered. The Democrats ran on the theme that John Marra was a "man's man" while I was the "evil Boss Paul." It got a little nasty. One of Rourke's candidates threw a softball at one of ours, and John Marra claimed somebody threw a cherry pie at him. I didn't believe that for a second. Anybody who has a cherry pie is just going to eat it!

Rourke's team hammered away on two issues: that we'd put the city at risk for liability by purchasing the power canals and that the public works equipment was insufficiently maintained.

I told Art De Fruscio, the new director of the Public Works Department, to clean up all the equipment and announce that we would put it all on display on Columbia Street that coming Saturday. We invited John Marra and all the Democratic candidates to inspect the equipment, along with the press. Seeing all that shiny equipment lined up turned out to be an impressive sight, but Marra never came. As for the tunnels, Dr. Jay invited Marra and his candidates to inspect them with him. Marra was again a no show, although Emma Shea and the media did come.

There were some violations during registration days, including harassment by county deputy sheriffs loyal to Dan O'Connell. Dr. Jay had to get the state's assistant attorneys general to chase the county cops out of town during the registration days. It was one of many battles in the run-up to Election Day.

CHAPTER THIRTY-SEVEN

BATTLE OF THE FLIERS

In September and October, we distributed ten citywide fliers, plus one for each ward candidate. Our slogan was, "Keep Cohoes an All-America City." Each flier outlined how we'd been keeping the promises we'd made in 1963. We also ran a "Know Your Mayor" feature, with photos of Dr. Jay in action, doing things like inspecting the tunnels and meeting with U.S. Congressmen. Dr. Jay's drumbeat was that his administration had accomplished more in forty-five months than the Machine had in forty years.

Rourke's fliers went a different way. Rourke copied our format and issued ten fliers, six of which were directly aimed at me. All of them accused me of pushing out Dawson so I could be the political boss and aired gripes about how I "purged" anyone who disagreed with me. They cut and pasted official letterheads together with phony letters purportedly written by me that described quid pro quo deals. Rourke's fliers featured what I called "deception scenarios," such as a picture of an abandoned, decrepit truck without its tires, with "Cohoes DPW – Department of Public Works" painted on the door. There was another flier with a photo of an abandoned building supposedly representing our lack of industrial development, although in reality the photo was taken before we had demolished the building as part of our urban blight mitigation efforts. Another flier showed a store with a "going out of business" sign on it to insinuate that our economic development program was failing.

A particularly low blow was a flier that showed a picture of equipment owned by my brother's construction firm sitting in front of the high school. Rourke was trying to imply that my brother was a benefactor of nepotism, but Tony, a Rensselaer Polytechnic Institute grad, had been the lowest bidder for a competitive project sponsored by the school district, not the city.

Such were the shenanigans Rourke pulled when most people did not know how to access public records, and before the digital age, when such lies would have been readily detected and fact-checked. Each flier ended with the tag line, "Elect a Man's Man for Mayor: Cohoes Citizens for John Marra."

To my surprise and delight, the Albany *Times Union* ran an editorial on the campaign, "If ever a political organization deserves the support of its community, the Citizens Party in Cohoes deserves this support. Their record of progress is clear. The Democratic record is one of obstructionisms and ill-disguised childish petulance."

The day before the election, *The Townsman*, a weekly newspaper in the north of the county, announced that the professional gamblers were giving odds that Marra would win. This was part of Rourke's deceptive strategy; they were printing his fliers.

In the end, Rourke's dirty tactics must have backfired. On election night, we celebrated a landslide victory of every municipal and county seat. Dr. Jay beat Marra, 7,140 votes to 2,960. This was far less than the 3,126 votes for Tom Carter, Willard Frament's Republican mayoral candidate in the 1959 election. We now had the entire city council.

The headline on the front page of the Albany *Times Union* read, "Citizens Sweep Cohoes." The article said we'd achieved the might of the once powerful Democrats.

But our successes never went unchallenged. Trouble was brewing.

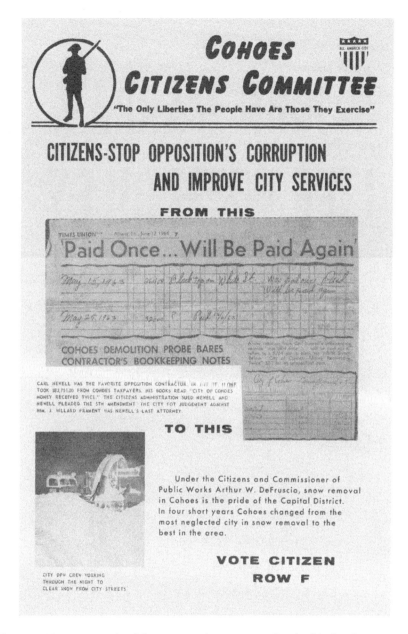

The 1967 Election "Battle of the Fliers". This Citizen's flier highlights the corruption under the machine and the lack of appropriate purchasing practices where their favorite vendor entered into his books, "Paid Once…Will Be Paid Again."

The 1967 Election opposition strategy created false pictures of our city deteriorating under Dr. Jay's administration. They showed a picture of the tennis courts behind the high school which belonged to the school district, not the city. Bill Riley was the Citizen's Chairman of the Recreation Commission.

KNOW YOUR MAYOR

MAYOR McDONALD EXAMINING THE TUNNEL FROM THE POWER CANALS UNDER ONTARIO ST. THE 1st MAYOR TO DO SO TO OUR KNOWLEDGE.

MAYOR McDONALD ALONG WITH ART DEFRUSCIO COMM. OF DPW, JOHN PERCY, CITY ENGINEER; PAUL VANBUSKIRK, ASSISTANT TO THE MAYOR; BOB CURRAN & FRANK COLURATOLO, CITIZEN ALDERMAN --- BRINGING THE BOAT DOWN THRU THE TUNNEL

"WHEN I RAN FOR MAYOR IN 1963, I TOLD THE PEOPLE OF COHOES THAT I WOULD DO ALL IN MY POWER TO FILL IN THE ABANDONED, RAT INFESTED, POLLUTED CANALS"

DR. JAMES F McDONALD, MAYOR

KNOW YOUR OPPOSITION

MISS EMMA A. SHEA - Has been on the common council since March 20, 1945 - when her political machine controlled Cohoes she voted yes on every ordinance (all 2365 of them) she voted "yes" on ordinance no. 46 for the year 1960. This ordinance allowed for the paving of Columbia St. by G. F. Wertime without competitive bidding to the tune of $100,000. When Citizen party brought political independence to Cohoes Emma Shea voted as follows: 1/2/64 voted against city purchases through state of New York.-- 6/23/64 defended William J. Dawson's purchase of city property at bargain rates --- ran as Dawson committee-man in 1st ward in 1964 primary.-- 1/19/65 voted against public hearing for new firehouse -- 6/18/65 voted against Cohoes parking authority -- 7/13/65 voted against utility tax to deprive city of funds-- 7/27/65 commended Donald F. Seaneol, a Republican for doing a fine job after Mayor McDonald removed him for dereliction of duty. The Appellate Division of the Supreme Court upheld Mayor McDonald.-- 11/23/65 voted against bond ordinance to fill in Cohoes Canals.--2/66 voted against 1966 city budget forcing city into financial straight jacket and mess for 7 months until States highest court ruled for Citizen budget.--2/7/67 voted against a raise for Arthur W. DeFruscio, a Democrat.--5/9/67 voted to give John F. Kelly $9,250.00. Appellate Division later said Kelly not to get a cent.

VOTE ROW F

A major issue in the 1967 Election, acquisition of canals from the Niagara Mohawk Power Company; the filling in and intercepting the domestic sewerage. This Citizen's flier shows Dr. Jay examining the roof of the tunnel that connects the canals with his team pulling a boat through the tunnels. The City Engineer stated that they would last another one hundred years.

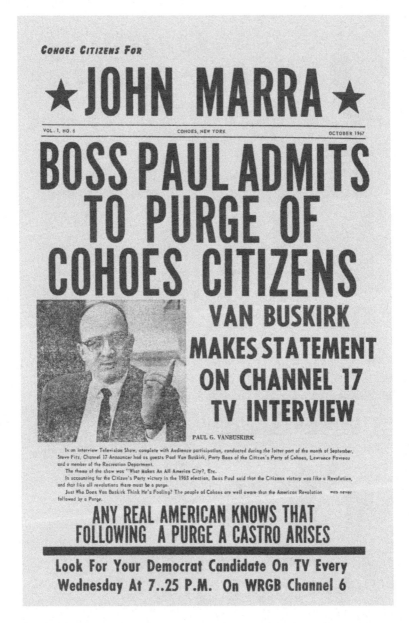

For the 1967 Election; Frank Rourke, copied our strategy from the 1963 Election, attacking me as "BOSS PAUL." His failed strategy attempted to portray me as an authoritarian and corrupt political boss. Since, six months earlier Cohoes was designated as an All-America City for getting rid of corruption

PART THREE:
REVERSAL

CHAPTER THIRTY-EIGHT

PAUL COUGHLIN LIVES OUTSIDE OF TOWN

Let me tell you a little bit about Paul Coughlin. He is one of the heroes of this story, and in a way, he still is. Paul and I worked together as reformers fighting many political battles during our first term. However, he had a serious drinking problem, which made our relationship difficult at times.

In the 1960s, Cohoes had fifty-six bars, one bar on average for every 375 man, woman, and child in town. Every single one of these establishments did a roaring trade. It may be part of the reason we were looked down upon by the rest of Albany County. We were always the butt of jokes, the kind that went like this: "My luck is bad, but at least I'm not from Cohoes."

Paul had gotten us to the State Court of Appeals four times and won all four cases, earning his reputation for brilliance throughout the Capital District, but he was afflicted by his drinking and had a turbulent marriage. Eventually and unfortunately, these things dragged him down.

One day I got a call from Paul. He asked if he could borrow $20 for groceries. I gave it to him and never got it back. I don't know why he didn't have the money; he was a successful lawyer, and Frannie, his wife, was a teacher.

Another time, Paul called me up, asking to borrow my car. "Paul, I got to have it back at four o'clock," I said.

"OK. I can do that," he said.

"What's wrong with your own car?" I asked him.

Apparently, his wife wouldn't let him take it. I don't know why. So Harold Reavey drove over behind me, I dropped my car off with Paul, reminding him he had to get it back to me at four o'clock, and headed back home.

Four o'clock came and went, no Coughlin. Five o'clock, no Coughlin. I called his house, and to my surprise, he answered.

"Paul, you're supposed to bring me back my car."

He cut me off, "Frannie won't let me bring your car down to you."

So, I had to call Harold again. We went back up to Coughlin's. The keys were still in the car, and Coughlin never showed up at the door, so we just left.

Then there was the time I had to pick Paul up to take him to a local television station. He'd just won an appellate court case in our favor, and a news program wanted to interview him. It was the same story as usual with Frannie not letting him have the car, so I had to pick him up. Halfway up his driveway, I stopped in my tracks. In the headlight beams, I saw a suit covered in tire marks laying across the dirt driveway. It's got tire marks across it. There's nobody in it, though.

I drove on and when I reached the door, Paul still wasn't dressed for his interview.

"Paul, you ready?" I asked him.

"We're not going. Look what she did to my suit."

"Oh, Christ. Get in the car. We'll get you a suit," I said, but he didn't move.

"Get in the car." I practically had to push him into the car.

I took him over to John Brady's house to borrow a suit. The sleeves came up to Paul's elbow. Brady was about five feet, four inches tall; Coughlin was six feet tall, easily.

I jokingly said to him, "Be sure the camera only shows you from the elbows up."

Paul would leave Frannie from time to time and, threatening divorce. Finally, when he did leave for good, he moved into a trailer up at Saratoga Lake. Frannie kept their car, so I let him use the city's car to get to and from work for a few days until he could buy his own. One day, he went to a bar after work, got drunk, and drove the city car into the Mohawk River. He managed to swim out. He got a hold of Pete Spadoni in the Parks Department, and Pete towed the car out of the water. He asked Pete to keep the accident under wraps, but Pete did the right thing and told me about it straight away.

We got Public Works to fix the car, and it was fine. But we had a liability on our hands, that much was certain. Adding fuel to the fire, Paul's trailer was outside the Cohoes city limits. This created a serious conflict.

CHAPTER THIRTY-NINE

GETTING CUT OUT

After the election, Coughlin asked to be made corporate counsel and wanted Dr. Jay to support his bid for it.

Stanton Ablett was doing a good job as corporate counsel. He took a lot of heat at council meetings, and he gave Coughlin free reign on the cases that he brought. I thought it was in poor taste for Paul to go after his boss's job. Plus, now that Paul lived outside the city limits, holding an appointed administrative position would have violated the city charter, which stipulated residency in the city.

There just wasn't any reason to remove Stanton Ablett, and I told Paul as much.

In truth, I didn't want Coughlin to be lead counsel because his drinking was getting out of control. Who would take us seriously seeing this guy up there, fighting for what's right, when the rest of the time he was getting into bar fights and beating the snot out of guys?

Bob Curran supported Coughlin's tough guy stance. Bob did not like Stan, didn't think he was aggressive enough. It was true that Stan came across as very mild-mannered, but he was thorough and deliberate, and with him, justice did prevail. Curran, Coughlin, and DeFruscio were having meetings up at Dr. Jay's house, lobbying for Paul to take his boss's job. They knew how I felt, so I didn't get invited to these meetings.

After the new term began, the mayor still hadn't appointed anyone to anything, not a single appointment. I'd ask him about it, and he'd say he didn't want to talk about it. Stan, being a "by-the-book" kind of guy, had been waiting to hear from Dr. Jay before returning to work. Finally, one day Stan asked me what was going on.

"Am I going to be reappointed?"

"According to the city charter, if an appointment is not made, the person currently occupying the position remains in that position," I told him. "Go back to work. Act normal. Don't worry about it."

Frank Brant, who'd became our police court judge after Landry resigned, also asked me the same thing when he still hadn't heard whether he'd been reappointed.

"Frank, you've got nothing to worry about."

He said, "What do you mean?"

I said, "Nobody wants your job." Of course, I was thinking, what the hell is going on with the mayor? He doesn't want to appoint anybody. I knew he wasn't going to reappoint Brady to city court judge because he and Brady had recently gotten into a public battle of words. He wasn't going to reappoint Harold Reavey for the Weights and Measures role because everyone said he wasn't doing his job properly. Then here was Coughlin, wanting to be appointed as the corporation counsel. Everything was in limbo. I think Dr. Jay's inaction was his way of telling everyone, "Leave me alone."

Once the new term started, I continued to be cut out of meetings. Previously, I would meet with the Common Council to go over their agenda. I was no longer invited to do that, and they didn't respond when I asked. I was being edged out more and more, and the press had started to report it.

CHAPTER FORTY

RESIGNATION: 1968

It didn't take long before Curran and the rest got word out to the papers that I was being excluded and losing influence. Meanwhile, Curran introduced an amendment to the city charter, removing the residency criteria for corporation counsel and paving the way for Coughlin's appointment.

Now I understood why they locked me out: they were planning an end run all along. But Dr. Jay would not get involved, didn't want to step into another fray. I think he'd had it after the whole thing with Turk, having to see the Senecal family being told that one of their own was not fit for his appointed office. That was hard on him.

For me, my dream-come-true of helping resurrect Cohoes was turning into a nightmare. First, there was the attempt on my life and the attacks on my character. Now, I was being shut out of the circle of people around the mayor. I was about to get hit even harder by Art DeFruscio. He told Curran that the Public Works Department had thousands in unpaid bills because there was no appropriation for a sewer job completed by my Uncle George. At the next council meeting, Curran demanded an investigation into whether I had engaged in nepotism. Naturally, the press had a ball.

Here's what had really happened. It had been almost a year since a representative from the State Health Department had come to see me about a problem in the nearby Town of Green Island. The Mohawk Paper Mill was dumping its effluent into the Champlain Canal, which was stagnant, so the organics had really started to stink. In response, Green Island was raising hell. The Health

Department wanted to know if the city could run a sewer line from the mill out to the Mohawk River. First, I wanted to know what the mill people had to say, so I requested a meeting with them.

A Mohawk Paper Mill chemist came to my office with a big jug of water. He tried to explain that there was nothing wrong with the effluent. "Have a look for yourself," he suggested.

What I saw were little white flakes, a byproduct of the paper-making process.

"This water is pure enough to drink," the mill chemist asserted.

"It is?" I asked. "Wait a minute," I said. I went to get a coffee mug. I took his water and poured it in the mug. "Have a sip," I told him. He wouldn't drink it.

So, I called back the guy from the State Health Department. Since Cohoes had a right of way across the Mohawk River, I thought it could be connected to the sewer line into the river. We couldn't create a new outlet into the river, though; that would be in violation of state law.

He retorted, "Don't worry about that. The governor will take care of it."

It was a small job, and at first DeFruscio told me that Public Works could take care of it. But after a little while, he said he couldn't get it done, but that he had talked to my Uncle George's employees, and they could do it for $9,000. Remember, anything under $10,000 didn't require bidding.

"If they can do it for $9,000, that's okay. Do you have it in your budget, though?" I asked him. He said he did, so I told him to go ahead and do it, and then I forgot about it.

George's guys sent DeFruscio a bill for nine grand, but Art never paid it, and he never showed it to me. After George's third attempt to settle the payment, DeFruscio brought it to Coughlin and told him there were $27,000 in unpaid bills due to my uncle.

Through the grapevine, I heard that Curran was going to make an issue out of it and was already figuring out what to tell the papers.

It was a Sunday night, and DeFruscio and Coughlin were over at Curran's house to go over the bills. Now, obviously, Paul knew it was the same invoice three times, so it was really only $9,000. Why hadn't DeFruscio ever paid it? And why was he making it out to be triple the cost? I didn't know, but now it looked like I had gotten my uncle—a guy I hardly talked to—on the city dole.

Then I recalled several months before when DeFruscio had tried to snare me in a trap. He came to my office and said some salesman had offered him a bribe. Art said he'd told him he'd first have to check with the political boss, meaning me.

I told Art to wait, and I'd be right back. I went down the hall to the police department and got Clarence, one of our plain clothes detectives. I sent him off with Art with instructions to tell the visitor that he was now talking to the boss. The guy again made an attempt at bribery, so Clarence arrested him. The guy ended up in jail until his bond came through. But I suspected Art was in on an attempt to frame me.

Not long after Curran and his gang had their Sunday evening meeting, Bill Riley and I were sitting together in the recreation office. It was next to the council's chambers, and we could hear Curran pontificating on how he wanted me investigated. I told Bill I was resigning.

"I don't blame you," Bill said.

I called Dr. Jay and told him. He was upset. He kept asking if we could get together with Curran and straighten things out. No way was I willing to do that anymore.

That night I wrote a twelve-page letter of resignation. I outlined everything I had done for the city and reaffirmed that I didn't deserve this kind of maltreatment. I also detailed exactly what had happened with Art and my uncle's company. I made sure to account for everything that had happened since I refused to support Coughlin for the counsel position. I said staunchly, "I support Stan Ablett. Coughlin wanted his job. Curran supports Coughlin. Coughlin is good friends with DeFruscio. They held a meeting at Curran's house and planned to humiliate me and push me out." It was all there in the letter.

The media loved it, but I was disgusted. Curran looked foolish, because he'd been exposed lobbying for Coughlin over Stanton. Stanton was a Democrat whose family had been in that city for years. He was well liked by both sides of the aisle.

Curran, meanwhile, was now revealed as the bad guy he was, but he blamed me. That was in February. We never spoke to each other again.

CHAPTER FORTY-ONE

THE TRANSITION

I never did work for Dr. Jay again at City Hall, a few months later, I returned to work, after Dr. Jay appointed me Director of the Cohoes's Model Cities' Program. My office was with the school district. The seeds I had sown in the fall of 1967 had come to fruition: we'd been chosen for the federal Model Cities Program demonstration project. It had been a long shot, with only 150 grants awarded nationwide.

News that we'd won reached Congressman Button. He, along with Dr. Jay, implored me to return for the duration of the year to write the five-year plan. Otherwise, the Congressman would not agree to back the grant, which he had to do for the Department of Housing and Urban Development to bestow it upon us. I accepted. First, we defeated an entrenched political machine. Second, we had won the All-America City Award. Third, we were federally designated as a "Model City." The work began in the spring and was to conclude a year and a half later in the fall of 1969. We had won the Triple Crown, as far as I was concerned.

It was a progressive program with two phases that would fund one year's work to create a five-year plan of programs and projects. If approved, it would provide us five years' worth of funding of up to 80% of the total cost of implementation. It would be a windfall for Cohoes. In a town like ours, which suffered from dilapidated mills, homes, and commercial buildings, the program would help us actualize the Citizens' objective of improving overall living conditions. I envisioned a comprehensive plan to overhaul social, economic, and structural issues in town that would start a cycle of inspiration, motivating citizens to participate in model citizenship and good governance.

Per the grant's requirements, I had to demonstrate that Cohoes had the capacity to carry out the program and could summon broad citizen participation. In the application, I delineated a Model Neighborhood Area (MNA) that included tracts where anti-poverty programs were already operating and where future programs were slated to launch. This included the mills, mill housing, and the central business district where the city was most established but deteriorating. Nearly three-quarters of the city's substandard housing was in these areas. They included a third of the adults over the age of twenty-five with less than eight years of education and more than half of the city's overall population. They were dense, poor, uneducated areas.

While I happily worked on creating the plan, the drama I had experienced largely subsided. The politicking within the Citizens Party continued, however, which distressed me.

During this time, something awful and unexpected happened.

CHAPTER FORTY-TWO

LOSING DR. JAY

I got a call from my friend, Bill Corbett, city treasurer.

"Dr. Jay has a brain tumor," he said.

I went to see Dr. Jay right away. Surgeons had removed the tumor, but the prognosis was that it would return.

Even Dr. Jay's ailments were not enough to stop the politicking and intrigue. Bob Curran was planning to introduce an ordinance that Frank Colaruotolo would take over as acting mayor since Dr. Jay was incapacitated. I knew that Dr. Jay would see this on TV, and that it would break his heart. Bill asked me if I had any papers requiring Dr. Jay's signature before he was pushed out of office. In fact, I had a request for a money drawdown for the Model Cities Program, which the Mayor had to sign. I took it over to the hospital and had Dr. Jay sign it. I passed it up the chain of command, and it served as proof that the mayor was still at work. That was the end of Curran's ordinance.

On June 22, 1969, at 1:20 a.m., Dr. Jay died. The doctors had expected him to live another year, but he died only three weeks after they removed the tumor. Before he passed, Dr. Jay told me he was at peace with himself. He said he was going to see his son Jimmy.

I spent the next several days with Virginia to help with the details of the wake, memorial, and cemetery burial.

The papers featured many well-written articles about Dr. Jay's medical, military, and public service history. I had lost a great doctor, friend, and political teammate. From 1961 to 1969, we had been the champions in our league.

St. Agnes Church held a celebrated mass for Dr. Jay. A delegation of mayors, medical professionals, and men and women from all walks of life came to pay their respects. Many people at the service had been delivered into the world by Dr. Jay. I accompanied Virginia to the mass and memorial. It was a depressing day; it was a depressing time.

Per the city charter, Frank Colaruotolo had replaced Bob Curran as President of the Council and was now acting mayor until a special election could be held later that November.

Petitions needed to be filed in September for the special election. The press reported that Eben Patrick, who had only been an alderman for six months, Frank Colaruotolo, and I were candidates. I don't know where they got their information; I had not been involved in party politics since the 1967 elections, and I was not interested in running. It was up to the Citizens Executive Committee to select the candidate. I thought that they should ask Virginia to run; with her in the role, it would diffuse power-playing.

Bill Corbett got a story to the press that the rank and file of the party wanted Virginia. It took hold and the momentum moved toward Virginia. There probably had been some jockeying for the nomination, but no one wanted to go public with their objectives so soon after Dr. Jay's death. The committee ultimately decided to run Virginia on the ballot.

I managed Virginia's campaign for the special election. We needed to demonstrate that she was a strong candidate. Congressman Button provided us an opportunity and arranged for Virginia to have breakfast with Gerald Ford, who was then the minority leader of the House of Representatives. This provided a photo op and a chance to discuss federal programs in Cohoes. Congressman Button also got two national unions to endorse Virginia. She was established as a credible candidate. Next, we

focused on her participation in the Model Cities planning committees and the Cohoes Community Center.

The Democrats threw their usual dirt, but Virginia was a tough
campaigner. At the Citizens Party citywide rally, Virginia said the
Democrats were running a vicious smear campaign and that voting
their ticket was "like betting on a horse that never won a race."

She won with 63% of the vote. The Citizens also won all
county supervisor seats. However, 500 fewer people voted in that
1969 off-year election than in the off-year election of 1965. The
Citizens Party was getting complacent.

CHAPTER FORTY-THREE

A COHOESIER REFLECTS ON HIS LIFE AND LENIN'S: 1969-1971

Not having to be concerned with what was happening in City Hall was easier than I thought. I thought I might miss the excitement of creating order out of chaos, devising innovative solutions for social and economic problems, as we had done by designing the Model Cities blueprint, but I found I could let it all go. It was time to hand over the program to the City Demonstration Agency, the Model Cities governing body created to select and hire staff to implement the plan.

I was now thirty-five years old. I had to admit to myself, my life had turned out pretty well. I had accomplished much since those cold winters growing up in that large, unheated Victorian home on Grant Street where I had taken care of my mother and earned my engineering degree—my ticket out of town, if I wanted it. Yet, after leaving City Hall, I had started to think that I could settle in Cohoes after all. I no longer felt my life was in danger; the Citizens Party was now in good hands with Jim Kellogg, a true reformer, as Chairman. I knew I could leave and easily find work further south where the weather was better, but RPI wanted me to help develop and teach an advanced degree program in urban and environmental studies. In the fall of 1969, I accepted the job.

My association with RPI had helped generate plenty of publicity and opportunities for me. The college had recognized my achievements in urban planning by featuring a few other alumni and me on the cover of its 150th anniversary catalog. While at RPI, I had also coauthored and published several well-cited papers on urban modeling with other RPI faculty. I traveled to various international cities on an RPI-funded grant to study different approaches to urban planning.

One of those cities was Moscow. It was 1970. It was a small coup for me, since this was during the Cold War. While there, I got to see one of the world's most successful political bosses of all time: Vladimir Lenin. He was dead, of course, but I got to spend some time alone with him. It was early on a Sunday morning. I awoke to aggressive knocking on my hotel door. It was Tanya, the young Soviet assigned to accompany me wherever I went.

"Paul, get up. Put on a suit and hurry."

It was hot, and I had had a few vodkas the night before, but I did as I was told. I didn't even have time to shower or shave. We hurried through the streets. I had no idea where we were headed until I started to hear the noise of the crowd. Soon, I could see it: Red Square, the place where every year on May 1, the Soviet Union held its impressive military parade. High-ranking Communist dignitaries would stand before the Kremlin Wall to view scores of rolling tanks and thousands of marching troops.

This was July, so there was no military parade, but there were thousands of citizens forming a line. Even now, thousands of citizens and tourists gather daily to pay their respects to Lenin, whose tomb is kept at Red Square. He has been lying there, preserved for all to see, since shortly after his death in 1924.

The throng was lined up about ten abreast. Tanya led me to the end of the line, just behind the Kremlin.

"Wait here. Do not go anywhere," she said and bolted.

It was getting hotter. I was in a suit and tie. I hadn't eaten any breakfast, and there were those vodkas from the night before. After about a half an hour and still no Tanya, I decided if she didn't return in another ten minutes, I was out of there. I was just about to leave when Tanya reappeared. "Come with me!" she ordered, dragging me by the arm. I started to panic a little bit, wondering about my status as an American in Soviet Russia.

Soon, Tanya steered me to the front of the line for Lenin.

"It is a privilege to be the first person to enter Lenin's Tomb," she said, smiling widely. "Usually, this is a privilege reserved for foreign dignitaries."

As I was the Kremlin's guest, nobody else would be allowed to enter the crypt until I had finished paying my respects to the great leader. Before I could enter, we had to wait for the changing of the guard and the official opening of the tomb for the day. When the clock on the Kremlin Wall struck the hour, the gate in the wall opened. Out came three soldiers, each holding a rifle by its stock and marching slowly in unison with high kick steps like the Rockettes at Radio City Hall in New York. The guards pushed open an enormous metal door. Armed soldiers lined both sides of the stairs all the way down to where Lenin lay in state.

Tanya and I descended into the crypt. Lenin was lying there in his glass covered coffin. He looked like he was taking a nap, dressed in his best clothes. I did not know what to do. Was I supposed to bless myself? After what seemed like minutes, Tanya asked me, "What do you think?"

I told her the truth, "He looks like a good friend of mine back home, Bill Riley. He used to run our Parks and Rec Department."

Tanya pushed me toward the exit. My time as a special guest of the Kremlin was up.

CHAPTER FORTY-FOUR

OUR MODEL CITIES
PROGRAM IN JEOPARDY:
1971-1972

Virginia called. She asked me if I would meet with her. It was March 1971. I hadn't talked to her in several months. It would be good to catch up and see how she had been faring since Jay's death and how she liked being mayor. I assumed she wanted to talk about whether to run for reelection and if I might want to help her run her campaign. I was wrong.

Instead, she confessed that the Model Cities staff put in place after I left hadn't managed to implement a single one of the sixteen projects called for under the first year action program. Worse, the Department of Housing and Urban Development had threatened to shut down the project and cancel the funding. Virginia had asked the Common Council for an ordinance to create a Planning and Development Agency to handle the situation.

"Paul, will you come back and run the agency, please?" Virginia asked.

I told her I would need a week to think about it. My first reaction was to decline. Bob Curran was still in the council and had voted against the Model Cities program, saying other cities were in more need than Cohoes. Eben Patrick and his cutthroat desire to be mayor was still an issue. And then there was Rourke, who was always "mobbing" and circling around City Hall. I found it depressing to think about their overall negativity when they didn't get their way.

However, thinking of the lost potential these projects had to truly improve the city was also depressing. Volunteers had devoted 2,000 hours of their time at workshops to develop the plan. To think of how negligence and ignorance could lead to the loss of all the federal and state funds we'd secured to create the Neighborhood Improvement and Urban Renewal programs, restore the opera house, build a Human Resource Center, develop the Erie Canal Trail, revitalize the Central Business District, and construct a public library would be senseless and tragic—something I would always regret if I didn't step up to the plate.

My friend and former Parks and Recreation Department Chairman, Bill Riley, now an engineer at a regional hospital, warned me not to go back. But I couldn't help but accept Virginia's offer. The next day in the paper, Bob Curran voiced his displeasure with Virginia's choice for director. The bitterness had subsided but had not washed away. The war was about to resume.

CHAPTER FORTY-FIVE

THE FAST TRACK

I could not have conceived what a mess the Model Cities Program had become. The planning committees were supposed to continue operating with their designated membership to meet their objectives, but the head of the Model City Agency and his staff had allowed the planning committees to disintegrate. More than half were not operational. Rather, politicians running for office were now on the committees. Many new members who were supposed to be residents of the MNA were not. The objective of the committees was to evaluate progress using metrics of the goals and objectives for their respective projects and recommend any course corrections. Program operations remained the responsibility of the operating agencies.

A prime example of how far the program had strayed was one program resident, who had spent many hours as Chairman of the Recreation Planning Committee, who was replaced by the Democratic candidate for mayor. It was clearly a political move, as the Democratic candidate was not even a resident of the designated program area. This prompted many of the original members to leave out of disgust and frustration. It all came as a surprise to me. There had been no oversight from Virginia, the council, or anyone else.

In addition, we were now two years behind schedule, and in order to keep the funding, we would have to put everything on the fast track. I was excited and humbled by the challenge: instead of five years, we had three at most to implement several large, difficult projects. It was city planning at its best.

I immediately contracted with professors at RPI's Management School to set up our management systems for fast-tracking the sixteen major projects. They identified required staffing, work task, timelines, and cost. They developed manuals for housing rehab and relocation activities. We also contracted with professors from the School of Architecture and Engineering.

I set up an organizational matrix. I hired one full-time attorney and one certified public accountant to serve all projects. I had one relocation staff and one technical staff. This provided numerous faster services at a lower cost.

I recruited a staff of eight for the Planning and Development Agency to serve all sixteen projects. For the Neighborhood Improvement Program (NIP), I hired Andy Loiselle. He was the only one to pass the civil service exam for building inspector and code enforcement. Andy was a high school dropout, but had proven skills as an electrician, plumber, and framer, and he understood how to work according to specifications and drawings. In addition, Andy would be serving people who were like him—not very educated or wealthy. He had a genuine rapport with people and was well liked. I planned to make him director of the NIP. He was the perfect fit.

Hiring Andy incited the rising new political machine. No sooner had I hired Andy than Eben Patrick, alderman from the First Ward, instructed me to appoint his friend Jim Cuva instead. I refused. He did not have the confidence of the people the program served. After having gone through what we had with Turk before, I knew better than to put an underqualified person on the make into a role that required public trust and competency. More upsetting to me was that Eben was demanding it in the first place. This smacked of the same kind of *Machine Politics* we'd fought against a decade ago.

When I appointed Mary Hebert to direct the relocation program, Eben was again upset. He wanted me to appoint a young woman just out of college. I refused because this job required real-world experience and problem-solving. If the building was uneconomical to rehabilitate, it would have to be demolished, resulting in complex repercussions, including moving residents. I had met Mary through the Model Cities Program. She had attended all of our committee meetings and had served on the one for relocation. She was smart, understood federal regulations, and like Andy, had a great rapport with the people she'd be serving. It made no difference; Eben Patrick decided I was the enemy.

I focused on what I had come to do, and over the next two years, I applied for and received millions in federal funds to acquire property, relocate businesses, and develop mixed-use commercial, residential, historical, and open spaces downtown. Some of the major projects were:

To rehabilitate 918 units, primarily in the old Harmony Mills brick housing in the First Ward. (This is a viable neighborhood today.)

To build the Erie Canal Trail that would thread together ten of the original locks as a greenway. Along the trail, we would construct four parks.

To establish a program for developers to pay only 50% of the cost for sewer and waterlines to encourage the private development of residential subdivisions and increase our tax base. Three large developments would result in 670 new housing units.

To open the ninety-five-unit senior citizen housing adjacent to the new community center and music hall in the Urban Renewal Area.

By 1973, we had done all this and much more in less than two years.

In order to work for the city, I had to give up my full-time position at RPI. But I loved my work, so I still found a way to teach. The college helped me create an important internship program for students earning their masters' degrees in city planning and management: students were given internships working on our Model Cities projects. The Peace Corps also requested that we train several of their recruits in housing rehab before they were sent to Brazil.

For me, one of the highlights was the restoration of the 475-seat Cohoes Music Hall using $700,000 of federal and state funds. It was one of the few restorable nineteenth century theaters on the east coast. It was constructed in 1874 and used as a theater until 1901. It hosted famous performers such as Buffalo Bill Cody, John Philip Sousa, General Tom Thumb, Eva Tanguay, and Cohoes native La Petite Adelaide. In 1968, I negotiated the purchase for $1. We were awarded the first grant under the new federal historic preservation legislation.

My grandfather's high school graduation ceremony was held there in 1888. The first performance after the restoration was held on March 7, 1975, hundred years after the original opening. It still hosts performances today.

When it was completed, after three phases of restoration, representatives from Housing and Urban Development (HUD) went on record saying it was the best preservation project they'd ever seen. The project even garnered the attention of *The Washington Times*. New York Governor Rockefeller called it an "architectural treasure."

We were up and running, and except for Councilman Patrick strong arming, things were going well. HUD had funded the year two and three programs. However, there remained the looming prospect of the next citywide elections in November. Who would be running the campaign, and what would be the results?

The development of the Model Cities first year action plan and 5 year plan of projects and programs involved over 100 volunteers on 16 committees that took part in five; all day weekend workshops at the new high school. Pictured above is one of the committees taking a break from their planning sessions (circa 1969).

The Dr. Jay McDonald Towers was the first housing project for low income seniors under the Model Cities Program and included a senior center adjacent to the Towers (circa 2018). It was located across from the Community Center.

This neighborhood shown above (circa 2018) was part of the Neighborhood Improvement Program (NIP). Today it is a viable neighborhood. It is where the mill homes are concentrated in Big Mike's 1st ward. The program provided grants and low interest loans for rehab, constructed new streets, curbs, sidewalks and tree planting

The Cohoes Music Hall (circa 2018, above) was one of our major historic restoration projects. Built in 1874 with a capacity of 475; the opening performance after restoration was held 100 years after the original opening. Today it is the City's cultural icon and still hosting performances. Gov. Nelson Rockefeller called it an "architectural treasure." The Cohoes Music Hall is on the National Register of Historic Places.

CHAPTER FORTY-SIX

OMINOUS SIGNS

It had been seven months since I had accepted the position as director of planning and development, a position created to ease the Department of Housing and Urban Development's concerns that all of our projects were staffed, producing, and performing. The Music Hall was under preservation. While I was conducting workshops for our Central Business District Plan, the mayor's office would send us the problems they could not solve.

By now it was 1971. Larry Favreau was running the Citizens Party campaign for council, assessors, and the county legislature. Virginia asked me to manage her campaign for the upcoming general election, and I agreed to help. Her motto was, "Our Platform Is Progress, Our Record Is Proof." She won with more than two-thirds of the vote.

Our Citizens Party Alderman candidate in the Third Ward lost to a Democrat who had employed an old strategy: vote for Virginia and give us a complimentary vote. The Citizens did not counter their strategy. All other Citizen Candidates took the Third Ward. The Citizens also won the three county legislators (reapportionment had reduced it from six to three), five seats on the city council, and two assessors.

Ernie Hatch had resigned as Third Ward alderman to run for county legislator and won. From this position, he became Chairman of the Physical Environment Committee established to support my projects. Ernie had helped get his brother Bob, a carpenter, appointed as the public works commissioner and had three other members of his family on the city payroll. There were whiffs of fresh corruption in the air.

The press described the election as reminiscent of the Party's 1963 victory, with several hundred jammed into the election night headquarters at St. Michael's Pavilion, but it wasn't really that way because the true reformers had moved on.

CHAPTER FORTY-SEVEN

THE STORM BREAKS: 1973

A reporter for the Albany *Times Union*, Joe Picci, once said, "Everybody in Cohoes wants to be Mayor." Not me. I wasn't looking for power. I wanted results. By the start of 1973, the Model Cities program was on track. I wrote and published a book about how we'd resurrected Cohoes using the Model Cities program. It was widely acclaimed within the industry and lauded by HUD. There was even a dinner held in my honor by citizens and friends throughout the community.

Not long after my book was published, Ernie Hatch burst into my office.

"Are you going to run for Mayor?"

"No," I replied frankly.

Ernie left as fast as he came in. I didn't even have the chance to ask him what his outburst was about.

Ernie was a former Marine. He was a reformer and was good with numbers and did the estimates for a local printing company used by the major magazine publishers in New York City.

A couple of weeks after he'd come to my office, Ernie was quoted in the press criticizing Virginia for her handling of the financial relationship between the city and the Model Cities program. In another article a few days later, he backtracked a bit. I did not pay much attention to the articles once he toned it down. I should have. He was laying down his planks to run for mayor, discrediting Virginia so that the party would back him instead.

In August, one of Ernie's relatives on the city payroll confided privately to me that Ernie had been telling people about a dossier "two feet high." He claimed it proved my mismanagement of the Model Cities projects, my many conflicts of interest, and my double talk. I told her not to worry because I knew we were clean.

"I know, but he can be mean," she said.

In August of that year, Virginia showed me a letter from Ernie demanding that she start screening applicants for city positions to ensure party loyalty as criteria for hire. In the letter, he'd warned against hiring a man whom he claimed had never had a kind word for the party. That and the fact that the man's father didn't like the party should disqualify him for hire. Whether Ernie was speaking for himself or acting as a spokesman for the party, I found out soon enough.

Jim Kellogg, now the Chairman of the Citizens Party, came to my office. He presented me with a letter from the party. It stated that I was to have any new Model Cities program hires vetted by the party first.

"Jim, this is what we fought against," I said.

He agreed. "But it's what the party wants. They voted on it," he said.

The party was more concerned with hiring people who were loyal to the party than they were about winning elections. The idea and motivation of changing Cohoes for the better was being supplanted by the goal of using politics as a vehicle for personal profit. The talk of the corruption in the Public Works Department and the Police Department was on the street. The Citizens Party was challenging our Civil Service Commissioner because they refused to sign the payroll for employees who were violating State Civil Service Rules and Regulations.

Not long after I had been named to run the Model Cities program, Yale University invited me to be a guest lecturer on our revolution and rise to an All-America City and the Model Cities program. When I had completed my talk, which had included a discussion about Senecal, Rourke, and Marra realigning with the Machine, the professor who'd invited me asked, "Do you know what you are telling me?"

"No," I replied.

"You're just trying to get everything you can possibly get done before your group turns out like the group you threw out," he said. It was a disappointing realization.

A few weeks after Jim Kellogg came to see me, Virginia asked me to attend a meeting requested by Paul Bourgeois. He had been a Citizens Party county legislator but now was an alderman. Professionally, Paul was a teacher now but had been a minor league ball player. He could be pleasant, but mostly he was mean with a reputation for saying nasty things about people.

When I asked what the meeting was about, she just said there were questions about my role with the Model Cities program. I took my assistant director, Bob Pawley, as a witness. Tom Donnelly, who was a council member from the Fourth Ward, also attended the meeting. I had a bad feeling about what was about to happen. Bourgeois' "questions" were about my attendance and punctuality. He said he'd heard that I was coming to work at 10:00 a.m. when the offices at City Hall opened at 9:00.

"Is this true, what I am hearing about your attendance?" he asked.

I told him that on occasion, that was probably true. On average, I had to attend two or three Model Cities-related evening meetings a week. Other nights, I met with Virginia to go over the details of those meetings.

"Have you got a problem with my performance?" I asked.

He didn't answer.

"It's my understanding that, so long as the work gets done, there are no particular hours for department heads," Tom offered.

After the meeting, Pawley said, "I cannot believe it. This is the way they treat you after all you have done for the city?" I told him that once the Model Cities projects were over, it was time for me to move on.

About a month or so later, Virginia called again to ask a favor. Ernie and Paul Bourgeois were running for reelection in November, but the County Board of Elections had rejected their poorly written petitions to be on the ballot. Virginia's assistant, Larry Favreau, had crafted them. Unlike Frank Landry, who had always been our secret weapon for writing unimpeachable petitions, Favreau was not meticulous enough to master the technical legalese required by the Board. Virginia wanted me to help save their campaigns. Harry Robinson, the city's corporation counsel, could have helped them. I wondered if he was secretly keeping his talents to himself, or whether he shared my concerns about Ernie and Bourgeois.

"I know you can think of a way they can get on the ballot," Virginia said to me after Favreau explained the situation.

I took my time before replying. I looked at Ernie. I read anger in his face. He knew that his political fate rested on me, a guy whom he reviled and sought to discredit. Bourgeois looked to me like he'd just scolded one of his students and now expected his cooperation. I stayed silent. I thought about how Ernie had been bragging about his dossier on me and how Bourgeois had upbraided me for coming in late for work. Even if I helped get them elected, I knew they would not stop their attacks on me, and they would have an even greater platform from which to lambast me to reporters.

Anger rose in me. Who were these people to turn the party exactly into what we'd fought against in 1963? They were entitled, self-absorbed, and immoral. They were hiding behind the very shield of reform politics that we'd put in place to defend against people just like them. They were not dedicated to public service and were making a mess of City Hall.

Virginia was a disappointment, too. I had learned from my time in politics that there are two types of corruption in politics. The first is a corrupt but iron-fisted leader, even if it's behind the scenes, like we'd had with Mike Smith. Now we had the second kind of corruption: a free-for-all by power players and squabbling factions because the leadership is too weak to rein it in. And so it was with Virginia and the manipulative men around her.

Favreau asked again if there was anything they could do to get back on the ballot. In fact, there was. Petitions could be filed within a three-week window. There were still three days before the deadline, plenty of time to get enough names on the petitions and refile. This was not a secret, but apparently even Favreau, the corporate counsel, had not bothered to learn the rules of the game.

"Sorry. I can't help you," I finally said. It was the final nail in the coffin. Ernie and Bourgeois missed the ballot and ran as write-in candidates. They got creamed. They lost their council seats and now had no county legislator. The press remained, however.

CHAPTER FORTY-EIGHT

A WAR ON ALL FRONTS

By 1973, objective reporters who knew the history and context of what the past decade had seen politically in Cohoes were long gone. Jim Dearborn, who'd covered the election of 1963, had gone to work for the FBI. Chuck Malley, who had studied at Syracuse University, and who'd covered the Cohoes municipal beat from 1965 to 1967, had moved to Alaska. Joe Picci, who'd covered Cohoes for the Albany *Times Union*, was now assigned the statewide politics beat. *The Troy Record* had been purchased by an outfit in Ohio. The new reporters were young, inexperienced, and underpaid. So were their editors. There was no longer the same commitment to the idea that they were locals just like the rest of us. And then there was Watergate. Everyone seemed to want to be the next Woodward and Bernstein.

Over the years, Cohoes had been home to a few celebrities like George Davis, a baseball Hall of Famer, and Mike Mazurki, a professional wrestler whose job as Mae West's bodyguard led to an acting career, but none of them had as high a local profile as I had and none at a time with such an agitated press.

Beginning with the success of our party's overthrow of Dawson's Machine, the All-America City Award, and my leadership of the Model Cities program, I had gained a reputation nationally, statewide, and locally. I had a number of accolades and accomplishments under my belt: I had published a book; I had chaired a two-day Congressional hearing on the effectiveness of federal aid programs in Albany's Capital District; I had testified before Congress about the benefits of the Model Cities program; and I had been the recipient of numerous awards for my work. This made me fair game. Except that the game wasn't fair. And like the elected and administrative officials now surrounding Virginia, the press suffered from a collective sense of entitlement built upon laziness.

They printed whatever Rourke—now out of office but still enraged that he had lost the 1967 election and his budget battle with me—and Ernie Hatch convinced them to print. Eventually, I had to hire a lawyer. There were accusations of mismanagement, conflicts of interest, and bossism, but a few stand out.

"Cohoes Pays for Material Not Used in City Project," was the headline. The September 26, 1973, article reported that 300 concrete blocks were ordered for the rehabilitation of an abandoned residential property on Summit Street, now owned by the city as part of the Neighborhood Improvement Project. The blocks—a $150 item in a line item for $15,000 of materials in its $1.5 million budget—were used for building the back porch, front porch, and entrance to a cellar. The reporter, Dan Hecker, reported that the 300 blocks had ended up somewhere else, but no one knew where. Hecker had never called me to get my side of the story, nor had he contacted Andy Loiselle, the project's program director. I don't know where he got his story. I called Andy and asked if all 300 blocks had been used in the building.

"Yes, Paul. I promise you. They were all used, and they are all there. Some are below grade, but they are all there," He assured me.

I told him to dig up around the porches to expose the blocks. Then I told him to mark and number each block and let me know if the 300 were accounted for. I called *The Troy Record*, the Albany *Times Union*, and the members of the Common Council. I told them all to meet me at the Summit Street property on Thursday morning if they wanted to see the numbered blocks to prove that the invoice matched.

Nobody showed up.

Along with the "unaccounted for cement blocks," Hecker had reported that, "Fourteen panels of wall covering were purchased and used to supply materials for a privately contracted job." The property was that of Mrs. Loretta Picard, another home being rehabbed through the Model Cities program. It was not a privately contracted job, so much as it was a public project for a private home, which is what the neighborhood improvement portion of the Model Cities program ultimately meant.

There had been a problem, however: the panels had been charged inadvertently to the Summit Street project. Andy said he would make the bookkeeping correction, but the innuendo that we were fronting for dirty dealing had been made, and the damage was done.

Two days later, Hecker published another report, still without ever having called me. The headline was, "Immediate Probe of Agency Asked" with the sub-headline, "Hatch cites: Van Buskirk's 'Misrepresentations'." Ernie Hatch, as Chair of the Physical Environmental Committee, was calling for an immediate investigation of my agency and me personally, to be conducted by the proper federal authorities. Hecker reported that the request for investigation had resulted from his previous report. He never reported that he'd been invited to count the blocks himself but hadn't bothered.

Andy and his attorney met with Hecker. Hecker insisted that the Diotte brothers, who were on a work program for the chronically unemployed, had informed him that no blocks had ever been delivered to Summit Street and that he had in his possession a copy of an invoice with Andy's signature for the blocks. In response, Andy produced a certified copy of the invoice from the block company. It was signed by John Diotte.

Both Diotte brothers were unskilled ex-convicts. More importantly, they were friends and neighbors of Ernie Hatch. I knew then that it was these two ex-cons who gave the story to Ernie, who'd in turn passed it to Hecker, who'd never bothered to vet it. Fortunately, a week later, Frank Colaruotolo, now President of the Common Council, did show up and reported to the press that there were more than 300 concrete blocks at the project.

Looking for their own Nixon, the three local television network affiliates were now sniffing around. The hunt for my head was on. A week later, the Albany *Times Union* featured an article by Donna Halvorsen, "Cohoes Records Missing for Contract Awarded to Van Buskirk's Uncle." The article claimed that a window on the door to the city clerk's office had been broken (actually it was the exterior window) during the night and that meeting minutes and contract documents were missing. The documents in question were for a meeting that had taken place nearly a decade before.

Broken windows and missing records. I knew Rourke was back, his 1967 election playbook in hand. Years later, Dave Bentley, a leader of the young Democrats, told me that Rourke confessed to breaking the clerk's office window to make the files on the fire house "go missing" but was concerned he'd be found out.

The next day Halvorsen ran another article about how in 1965, Dr. Jay prevented Turk Senecal from switching his vote to award a public works project to the lowest bidder, resulting in my Uncle George getting the business instead. There was even a picture of Turk.

The evening edition of *The Troy Record* dug deeper and found the meeting minutes that proved Halvorsen's story untrue. Neither paper bothered to mention that Turk had been found guilty of two counts of dereliction of duty as public works commissioner, nor that he'd run for public office and had been soundly rejected by 84% of voters.

The Troy Record surprised me the next day. On the editorial page was a letter from Virginia: "A review of recent newspaper articles does, in my opinion, prove beyond a reasonable doubt that they are the work of irresponsible political opponents and an irresponsible press. The newspaper reports are being passed on to the people of Cohoes as factual reporting when in truth they contain misstatements and deceptions."

I appreciated what Virginia had tried to do, but things only got worse.

CHAPTER FORTY-NINE

NAÏVETÉ AND POLITICS

"That stupid son of a bitch! Where in hell are his brains?" That was the question I had to ask about Andy Loiselle, the guy I had hired to run the NIP, when his assistant called to let me know what his boss had done.

Andy had taken some work-training program personnel, the Diotte brothers, down to the old mill apartments on Olmsted Street that I owned and was rehabbing. Andy was showing them how to frame a door, part of their training. I had already accepted bids and chosen contractors for all the necessary carpentry, plumbing, and electrical work to be done. Andy's brother was doing the carpentry. This latest incident was bound to hit the papers in the most twisted way.

I immediately walked the two blocks to the apartments.

"Get the hell out of here. This is private property and you are trespassing!" I yelled at them. They scrambled out of there, but there was no avoiding what was to come.

The Troy Record reported that work-training personnel were doing the full rehab of my apartments, not just the carpentry but the electrical and plumbing as well. They included the weird, untrue detail that I had purchased the properties with my mother's money and I had been a "consultant for the White House, federal agencies, and city governments."

I had never been a government consultant. That made me sound like a lobbyist. I had only ever been an appointee or civil employee. For the dime store novel touch, the article also stated,

"When a car was available, and he had enough money to buy cigarettes, he toured his projects."

The reports reminded me of something: the strange fabrications Rourke had written in the fliers he'd distributed in the 1967 elections. And in any case, I had a car, and, on my salary, I could afford cigarettes.

The bizarre accusations went on, but the most off-the-wall statement that *The Troy Record* printed was that I was so poor I had frequently showed up to the mayor's house begging for food. Where were the adults in the local papers, and who was letting these fantasy tales go to press?

CHAPTER FIFTY

TINKER TO EVERS
TO CHANCE

In the early 1900s, the Chicago Cubs' shortstop Joe Tinker, second baseman Johnny Evers, and first baseman Frank Chance were like a machine. Their seamlessly thrown double plays across the infield were legendary. "Words, those are heavy with nothing but trouble: Tinker to Evers to Chance," goes the famous poem about the team.

It was starting to feel to me like the press, Eben Patrick, and Ernie Hatch were teaming up to throw me out every time I tried to advance the play, which is to say, just to do my job.

The Troy Record refused to admit the "Missing 300 Blocks" story was based on false information. It seemed designed to give Ernie Hatch an opportunity to call for an investigation of my agency. Ernie was setting me up so Eben could discredit me and have a platform to run on for mayor.

A new round of articles about me started appearing in the papers, this time saying I was mismanaging the Model Cities program. Eben was repeatedly quoted saying the council had hired a private detective and an attorney to investigate me. This was illegal—they would have needed an ordinance and appropriations to do this, which they didn't have. They ignored the rule of law like the Machine did. Eben announced in the papers that "a full-report into the mismanagement of the Model Cities program by Paul Van Buskirk" would be forthcoming.

I got wind of a scheme that Patrick had urged the Common Council President, Frank Colaruotolo, into asking the feds to investigate my agency. Frank complied and sent a letter to the feds to have my projects investigated. I preempted him by sending a letter to the regional administrator of the federal Department of Housing and Urban Development to explain that vicious local politicking was threatening the program, and I asked him to conduct an audit of my agency "to preserve the high quality of programs and to protect the integrity...of the good people who staff them." I sent a copy to Colaruotolo to have it read to the Common Council members. I wanted to make it clear that I had nothing to hide.

Next, Eben passed the ball to Jim Cuva, a crony he jockeyed into the Citizens Party's chairmanship after Jim Kellogg left. Cuva started giving interviews to the press, saying that the party's Executive Committee was going to have a vote on whether to tell the mayor to fire me. Soon, the local media was reporting that the party's Executive Committee had voted 16 to 1 to have me fired. I wondered who the one person was, brave soul. Whoever it was didn't stay lonely long: days later, an article ran saying the mayor was going to quit if the Citizens Party members did not back Van Buskirk.

Then the papers all reported Cuva saying a revote had resulted in the committee backing me 10 to 9, never mind that the math was wrong. Months later, the press reported that Paul Bourgeois, a member of the Executive Committee, said the vote never took place. So much for the press conducting its due diligence.

I called Colaruotolo. "What the hell is going on?"

"Well, I got a lotta questions, Paul," he said coyly.

"What are they?" I asked.

"Your properties on Olmstead Street are included in the Comprehensive Plan."

I didn't have a reply. I was too stupefied for a moment. It was now dawning on me these people did not really understand how the program worked, and that the papers had never bothered to explain it, even though it was a major initiative in town. Still, the comprehensive plan was a public document. It had been presented to the Common Council in 1967. It was routinely updated to show the current condition of housing stock and recommended future land use and current zoning.

"Frank, the whole city is in the comprehensive plan, including your beer business," I told him. So much for his being a potential ally. He didn't even understand what was happening.

I then called Tom Donnelly, Fourth Ward alderman.

"Tom, what the hell is going on here?"

He said, "Paul, I told these guys, they are destroying the Citizens Party."

I called Irene Rivet, Second Ward alderman.

"Paul, all I can tell you is that I will do whatever Virginia wants me to do."

None of them could tell me the specifics of what I had supposedly mismanaged. I told them all I was innocent, and I asked them to go through all the program's files, including the press. "Do whatever you want to do. I don't care," I said to all of them.

Even if they did, I knew I was now on my own and couldn't trust anyone, so I kept duplicate files in my office under lock and key. That way, if any of the program's files suddenly disappeared or were altered, I could prove them wrong. I knew our programs were clean and well managed, since we had to follow hundreds of federal rules and regulations to be funded.

I asked the Albany *Times Union*, "Why are your people after me? Why don't you go after Public Works? That's where all the corruption is."

The corruption in Public Works was well known on the street. The reporter there said, "Well, give us documentation, or some information," as if that had ever been their standard before.

I said, "Sure, I will talk to you, but only off the record."

"We don't go off the record," the reporter told me. "Then you don't get the information because I know if I'm not going off the record the ones out to destroy me are just going to say it's political."

I was fed up. All I had asked of Virginia was to be left alone to fast-track the projects. My only aim was to accomplish the things no one else had known how to do, but here were these political power players coming after me. They were now in control of the party apparatus. They controlled the Common Council. Jim Cuva, who had never espoused any of the principals of our party, was now the Citizens Party Chairman. Cuva was Eben's inside guy. It meant that just like the old Dawson days, Eben Patrick was the one who really controlled the party and now the party was coming after me.

When I founded and grew the party, it was for the purpose of ending corruption, not attacking innocent people. Now, the mayor and department heads were receiving letters telling them that any hires must be vetted and approved by the Citizens Party, as if there were no Civil Service laws. Some members of the Citizens Party Executive Committee, the ward leaders, and district committeemen were on the city payroll, as were a growing number of their relatives and friends. It was 1962 all over again.

CHAPTER FIFTY-ONE

PUSHING BACK

I went to a local attorney, Frank Carroll. I gave him clippings of all the slanderous articles and chronicled all the events leading up to the investigation against me.

"They don't want to get rid of you," Frank told me. "They want to destroy you. We could win on libel and slander, but we can't prove damages, and it will cost you tens of thousands of dollars."

For $5,000—about $40,000 in today's money—I hired him on retainer. Then I went into offensive mode with Frank as my cover.

I had hired a lot of RPI graduates to work in the Model Cities program because I knew that they had the correct technical education. One of those hires was a brilliant former student of mine. I had mentored him and was pleased to have him on staff. Then one day, he didn't show up for work. It turned out he had another job the whole time as a contractor for the U.S. Coast Guard. His other job was based out of the State Senate in Albany, and he had been using Model Cities secretaries to write reports for his contract work. I confronted him as soon as I found out, and he quit. He and another guy I'd fired for regular absence started feeding the press a lot of garbage about how the NIP was overrunning costs and that the department was playing fast and loose with allocating materials meant for one project into other buildings instead.

Then, my former student decided to sue me for half a million bucks. I asked Frank Carroll, "How can he sue me for half a million dollars? Is it that easy?"

He said, "Yes, it's that easy."

I said, "Then, let's sue him."

He said, "Yes, we can sue him. How much do you want to sue him for?"

I said, "Make it $750,000."

So that's what we did.

Eventually, he contacted me about a détente. We agreed that if he dropped his suit, I'd drop mine, and that was that. As for the papers, I took matters into my own hands. They continued to come after me, paying no attention to the flagrant abuses of Hatch and his henchmen.

Ernie had several family members on the city payroll. There was Bob Hatch as commissioner of Public Works. Ernie's stepson, who knew even less about Public Works than Bob, was working in the department, too. Ernie's wife was the head of data processing, though she was very good at the job and a valued employee. She stayed in that position until 2000.

The same person who'd tipped me off about the two-foot dossier also confided in me that Ernie Hatch hadn't paid his income tax for seven years. I told my assistant, Bob Pawley, about it. Bob was no fan of Ernie either. He turned Ernie into the IRS. Soon, Ernie was under federal investigation, which thankfully drew his attention away from attacking me.

This gave me a little breathing room. Now I could put a stake in the heart of the bogus investigation into my programs. I presented a CPA's audits I'd requested of our projects for the Model City Year 3 and the Summit Street project to the committee. The proof was there: we had a $9,250 surplus.

Board member George Robinson said, "This information I think is what everybody wanted. In view of these reports," he asked Ernie, "is there any need for an investigation?"

"It is shy of the information the committee had asked for," Ernie said, but no one from his committee had ever asked me for anything specific.

Going into the meeting, the press had played it up as a shoot-out between the Physical Environment Committee and the Model Cities program with Ernie Hatch and Paul Van Buskirk slinging their guns. After the meeting, the reporters wrote that Ernie had failed to ask me the hard questions. They apparently hadn't asked him any either, or they would have realized that he had no case.

The election of officers for the Physical Environment Committee was also conducted at the meeting. I was unanimously elected to succeed Ernie as Chairman. That was the last of Ernie's courtship of the media.

Eben Patrick continued his relentless attacks on me, however. He introduced an ordinance to curb the spending of the Planning and Development Agency, stating that Common Council was ultimately responsible for the management of the city's money. This was not true. According to the city charter, the Board of Estimate and Apportionment has the responsibility for managing the city's money. So much for the rule of law.

I did what the newspapers should have done. Using the city's 1972 budget and financial statement, I conducted an analysis of all nineteen city departments, including Patrick's Common Council. Using these publicly available documents, I showed that the city had overspent its budget by $76,500. The Public Works Department—the Hatch family stronghold—alone had overspent $60,678. I told Patrick he needed to investigate several departments, including his council, for overspending. I delivered my analysis to Eben, the reporters, and Virginia. Nothing happened, except that Patrick continued to discredit me, saying he was sure their private investigator's report would show I was mismanaging the funds.

Next, I went after Cuva. Under the Hatch Act, federal employees or those supported by federal funds are prohibited from participating in political activities. This had not applied to the Citizens Party during the 1963 and 1967 elections because independent parties were exempt. It wasn't until 1970 that the law changed to include independent parties. Since Patrick had Cuva appointed Assistant Urban Renewal Director, and was being paid with federal funds, and as Chairman of the Citizens Party, he was in violation of the Hatch Act. I had Frank Carroll file a complaint with the Federal Civil Service Commission. The feds investigated and Cuva resigned from his urban renewal position.

My momentum was boosted further when Art DeFruscio, the old Public Works Commissioner, delivered some unexpected ammo. He called me to say that a number of employees in the Public Works Department were fed up with its Director, Bob Hatch, Ernie's brother. They were willing to sign affidavits about rampant corruption inside the department.

Art agreed that he would get his guys to meet with me in the back room of John's Grill, down by the railroad tracks. Bob Pawley, my assistant, brought a typewriter. One by one, as each worker told his story, Bob typed it all up. Bob was also a Notary Public, so after he typed up each one, he read it back to the guy. If it was correct, Bob had the guy sign it. Then Bob signed it, sealed it, and by the end of the night, we had twenty-seven official affidavits of corruption. Most of them dealt with misuse of city funds, materials, and labor for private use, the very thing Ernie had tried to accuse me of. The abuses ranged from a city official having city employees and material delivered to their camp in the Adirondacks to a member of the Common Council having city employees work on their vehicles. The corruption was blatant, even worse than under Machine rule.

I gave copies of the affidavits and other information to Virginia and her corporation counsel, Harry Robinson, and waited for their response.

CHAPTER FIFTY-TWO

BROKEN WINDOW
DÉJÀ VU

I received an early morning phone call in my office from Andy Loiselle that someone had broken in through a window in the NIP's office and gone through the files. Now, the Loretta Picard file was missing. Broken windows again. Sounded like Frank Rourke. This time I was ready for him.

I told Andy what to expect: the press would have been called by the rock thrower and reporters would be showing up soon looking for that file. I told him to tell whoever showed up that the files were in my office. That was where I kept all the duplicates of the NIP that I knew would be essential. Andy said, "They are at the door now," and quickly hung up.

An hour later, the reporters from the Albany *Times Union* arrived at my office. I was waiting for them. It was the same reporters as before: Donna Halvorson and Jerald Budgar. I told them to look at anything they wanted. They went through the file cabinet. No missing file. No story. In my mind's eye, I could see Rourke's face when the reporters told him they'd seen the file, when Rourke probably had it in his hand. Halvorson and Budgar stood there looking annoyed, as grim as morticians. I used to call them the embalmers.

"All my programs are under budget, and you are reporting that I'm over budget. Why don't you look at the facts?" I pressed them.

"This has got nothing to do with that," Jerald said.

They were determined to discredit me, period. Frank Carroll, my lawyer, had said that they were out to destroy me, and he was right. Frank sent the Common Council's attorneys implicit warning to be careful how they proceeded with their attacks. It was a brief debunking of each false news story, detail by detail. He sent copies to the editors of the local papers.

CHAPTER FIFTY-THREE

MEET THE PRESS

Two months passed, and nothing had been done with the affidavits. I met with Virginia and asked her why she'd not done anything with the proof of corruption I had given her. "The Public Works Department is more than $60,000 over budget!" I exclaimed.

"You met at a bar when they signed those affidavits. You got them drunk and then they gave their statements. I can't use these," Virginia told me. She looked at me, almost daring me to challenge her. I didn't. What she was accusing me of was not true, and she knew it. She wasn't equipped to handle these kinds of conflicts. She didn't know how to push back. She was being run by the party. I was on my own.

I decided to show the papers what it felt like to be the one on the bad end of baseless stories. If the first-string Cohoes beat reporters were going to pretend that they were Woodward and Bernstein, I would wait until the night shift.

It was near midnight. I called the Albany *Times Union* and, in a disguised voice, asked for the Cohoes desk. After a brief hold, I was put on the line with a reporter. Speaking as though I were an employee in the Public Works Department, I told him about city employees making Bob Hatch's kitchen cabinets in the basement of the City Hall, having then painted and installed in Bob's house; and I told him if he wrote a good article, I would call him again and give him more stories.

He was thorough. He got the names of the other employees involved and verified what I had told him. The paper ran the story. We developed a relationship. I fed him information from the affidavits, he sought collaboration, and the stories got published. At last, the editors and reporters turned their attention away from me and onto the Hatches. Several pieces appeared exploring whether Bob Hatch should or would resign. If so, who would replace him? *The Troy Record* wrote that there were only two logical candidates: James Cuva or Paul Van Buskirk. Mayor Virginia received a petition signed by twenty-seven public works employees requesting her to appoint me. I publicly stated I did not want the job.

I wanted nothing more to do with politics in that town, but I wasn't done knocking these guys out of their canoes. I suspected that the Albany *Times Union* would run virtually any negative story about me without bothering to verify the source or the facts if they thought it would sell papers. I decided to test my theory.

Again, I worked the night shift crew. I called asking for the Cohoes desk, using a different voice than I had used before. I told the guy on the phone that I had just left a watering hole near City Hall and I had seen Van Buskirk taking files out of his office and putting them in a pickup truck.

"You'd better get a photographer up there right away!" I told him. I wasn't there, so I don't know if they ever sent a photographer, but the next morning, there was an article saying I had been seen the night before taking files out of City Hall and packing them into the bed of a pickup truck. Days later, I asked a Albany *Times Union* reporter where they got the information.

"Verified sources," he said.

When I had called them in disguise, the guy had never even asked my name! I was now convinced that anyone could call the Albany *Times Union* with a derogatory story about me, and it would find its way into print with no vetting. The press has the power to destroy an innocent person's reputation. They knew it, and they abused that power for profit. The paper was as morally corrupt as Dawson and the rest of the Machine.

So I went after *The Troy Record*, too, hoping to shed light on their shoddy journalism. There was a race going on between the Albany *Times Union* and *The Troy Record* as to who was going to destroy me first. Between the Albany and Troy papers, I had five journalists reporting on me. That was more coverage than the governor had.

Again, I called at night and asked for the Cohoes desk. This time, I told them I was a clerk at the Cohoes branch of the State Bank. I said Van Buskirk had been in that day to close out his account, and I had heard that he was leaving town altogether. I said if they wanted to check out my story, they could call the bank's manager, Hank Vogel. I knew if they called Hank, he would have to say he could not comment on customers.

I hung up. A few minutes went by. The phone in my apartment rang. It was the reporter from *The Troy Record*.

"Is Paul Van Buskirk there?" he asked.

"Who? I just moved in here. I don't know any Van Buskirk. I don't have time to talk to you; I'm busy moving in furniture," I lied. I knew I had to get out of the apartment before the reporter arrived to knock on the door. I had been dating a lovely woman in town whom I later married, so I called her. Nancy let me stay the night. When I got there, I called Bob Pawley and told him the story. When he finished laughing, he hung up, called *The Troy Record*, and asked for the Cohoes desk. He told the reporter he was a janitor at the airport. He knew who this guy Van Buskirk was and thought it was strange he was at the bar there, talking with another guy, telling him he was flying to Kennedy so he could catch a flight to Guatemala. The reporter asked Bob if he could keep me at the bar until he and a photographer could get there. When they arrived, no one was there.

Instead, the next morning they had a reporter at my office door. I told my assistant to say I was supposed to be there but that

I'd never showed up. I went to work the day after that. No story ever appeared. They knew they'd been beaten at their own game.

CHAPTER FIFTY-FOUR

A FAREWELL TO POLITICS: 1974

It was already Christmas. The papers all said the Council's report on the investigation into me would be published any day now. I sent several letters to Frank Coloruatolo and Virginia, requesting to see a copy of the report. All of my letters went unanswered.

I tried to smoke them out. Since I knew now for certain that the papers would print anything, I told them I knew that there was no report. It was a hoax. Nothing existed. I knew they had nothing. After making so much noise, they knew they could not create a plausible story of mismanagement, so their game was to delay, delay, and delay in the hopes that someone involved in my projects would screw up.

In January, the gig was finally up. The private investigator the council hired to investigate me—without authorization and proper appropriations—sent both of the papers a letter with his findings. He could find no evidence of corruption. He wrote, "I had never met nor heard of Mr. Van Buskirk prior to this time, but recently I have heard some very fine things about this gentleman...I hope that he will accept this apology."

I took stock. All my projects were finished or close to being finished. Congress had just passed legislation to transform the project funding to a revenue sharing model. This meant that Cohoes was guaranteed funding for years four and five, but after that, they would need to compete against other cities for grants. The Model Cities Planning Committee in Cohoes was now so politicized that any time there was a new appointee, the papers would identify their political party affiliation. Often, the appointments were made in violation of federal law, since the persons on the board were supposed to be residents of the MNA. Now, half the committees were inactive, and our local Model City Agency's administration and all its processes were in chaos.

The city administration under Virginia's leadership was in disorder, plagued by weak department heads and multiple scandals. The latest humiliation involved the commissioner of public safety: he had hired his nephew as a police officer, who was now reportedly threatening women with arrest if they did not have sex with him.

The council had no respect for the rule of law. It was just like it had been in the Dawson era. The reformers were gone: Dr. Jay, Bill Riley, Frank Landry, Stanton Ablett, Ralph Robinson, and Frank Bourgeois. Even Bob Curran and Paul Coughlin before they become power players.

The press would not relent in its war to destroy my reputation, just as my attorney Frank Carroll had predicted.

I reflected on my favorite novel, Hemingway's A Farewell to Arms. The protagonist is an American volunteer army ambulance driver stationed in Italy among the Allies in World War I. The soldiers accuse him of something he has not done. He has dedicated his life to the Allies' cause, but now they want to execute him. He escapes before they can kill him and deserts the army altogether. He feels guilty but concludes that when the ones you want to help want to kill you, it's time to move on.

I'd been composing a letter in my head for a while. It was time to sit down and write it. In the letter, I reviewed all the years I'd been actively working with a group of dedicated reformers to turn the city from a depressed and dying mill town into a place of hope—something possible only with the help of "doers," until we were overrun with "non-doers." I reviewed the character assassination attempts I had endured and reflected on how even if they had not destroyed me, they had destroyed my ability to function effectively and to fulfill the hopes and dreams of the people of Cohoes through the agency's programs.

It was twelve pages long, even after I edited it. It was addressed to Virginia, but I decided to deliver it in tandem with a press conference held at my attorney's office. The papers and even the local television stations were all there.

The Merchants and other groups placed open letters to me in *The Troy Record* asking me to reconsider. The Merchants' letter stated, "We want to reaffirm our previous expressions of gratitude and appreciation of your efforts on behalf of the city...In our past activities we have always found you to be a dedicated public servant whose enthusiasm, integrity and knowledge have been an inspiration to those associated with you. We ask that you continue your efforts with the same zeal you have shown in the past." The Senior Citizens gave me an award for my contribution in establishing the Senior Center and for getting program funding.

The Albany *Times Union*'s response was to run an article accusing me of my having put the groups up to it to save my job. Christ, I could not wait to get the hell out of this snake pit. Eben Patrick told the director of the Merchants and the Senior Citizens if they published the letter and gave me an award, "they will live to regret it." The old machine tactics.

I completed a final audit of all of our programs and projects to date and, with proof that all was in order, presented them to the Mayor. On January 31, 1974, I walked out the door to City Hall and moved on with my life. It was fourteen years of political harassment and civic accomplishments. It was my farewell to politics.

POSTSCRIPT

In May of 1974, the council's report on its investigation into me was released. It stated:

"...The investigation did not reveal any evidence of wrong-doing...under the specific circumstances, there were no violations of conflict of interest laws...The investigation covered all allegations mentioned in the press, general, and some individual activities in particular."

Ernie Tetrault, the six o'clock news anchor on our local channel, said it best, "Paul Van Buskirk said they would not find anything because there was nothing to find, and they did not."

Case closed. For me, the war was over. As for the rest...

Citizens Party: In the next citywide election in November 1975, the Citizens Party lost the mayoral vote, four council seats, both assessors, and all three county legislature seats. City Hall was now returned to the hands of the Cohoes Democratic Party, still subservient to Dan O'Connell. The Citizens Party once again failed to target the necessary voter populations. After this loss, the Citizens never did return to City Hall and eventually ceased to exist altogether.

Dr. Jay McDonald: He was our icon, our standard bearer who supported all of our reform programs. He was a war hero, too, as well as a medical doctor for the poor. And, he was my friend. There will never be another Dr. Jay. A plaque dedicated to Dr. Jay, describing him as a public servant and humanitarian, was placed in the lobby of City Hall but was taken down by a Democratic administration.

Virginia McDonald: After her defeat in 1975, she remained in civic affairs and spent time visiting her granddaughter in California. After I left in January 1974, I never saw or heard from Virginia again. She died at the age of eighty-six in 1999.

Paul Coughlin: I consider Paul one of the heroes of this story. He was a brilliant attorney, but he was unpredictable. In 1968, he'd been appointed Chief Counsel for the New York State Pure Water Authority. It was a prestigious position. He left the job about ten years later. After that, he worked sporadically and eventually became a nomad living in an old Volkswagen bus. He mostly stayed in Key West. He'd come to visit me from time to time where I lived in Florida, and we'd talk about the old days. He died in 1995. He was sixty-nine.

Frank Rourke: He remained with the Cohoes Democratic Party. He tried to create the impression that he'd strategized the Democrats' campaign to win the 1975 citywide election, though I heard otherwise from Democratic insiders. Rourke described in the press the organizational meeting when the Democrats took power in 1975 as "beautiful, and his best ever." He died two years later the age of forty-seven. His obituary referred to him as a cofounder of the Citizens Party.

Turk Senecal: Shortly before his death, Rourke had lobbied the Democrats now in City Hall to once again appoint Turk commissioner of Public Works. It worked. The new mayor reinstalled Turk. Ten years later, Senecal was nabbed by the FBI for accepting bribes in a statewide investigation. He was convicted of embezzling $25,000 from the city. In February 1991, Turk was sentenced to six months in the federal penitentiary, fined $25,000, and given a year of probation. He appealed, ended up serving community time, and paid the city the $25,000 he took in bribes, before moving to Florida, where he lived until his death in 2014.

Eben Patrick: In 1979, he got his wish to run for mayor on the Citizens Party ticket. Jim Cuva was his Campaign Manager. Cuva had the nerve to ask me for my help running Patrick's campaign; he wanted to know what strategy he should use. Patrick ran with a full ticket, suffering the worst defeat of any Cohoes major candidate for mayor; he was repudiated by the people of Cohoes by receiving only 22% of the total vote. Cuva lived to be ninety, and Patrick died at eighty-three.

Ernie Hatch: He worked for the Cohoes Democratic Party in the 1975 election. The IRS's investigation into his tax fraud ended his political career, however. Ernie moved to Albany, where he died in 1996 at the age of sixty-five.

Bob Hatch: In the fall of 1974, Virginia finally took my accusations of corruption seriously and had Bob Hatch, Ernie's brother and her Commissioner of Public Works, investigated. Instead, Bob resigned. A month later, at a Board of Estimate and Apportionment meeting, Frank Colaruotolo as Common Council President introduced a motion to hire Bob Hatch as a consultant to the Public Works Department to help prepare the budget. His consulting fee was the same as his salary had been as commissioner.

Frank Colaruotolo: Frank retired from a successful career as a small businessman. He died in January of 2020.

Harold Reavey: Harold became disenchanted and left the party in 1968. I talked to him throughout his life until the day he died, at age fifty-three, of kidney failure, at the same age and from the same disease as his mother.

Bob Curran: After the 1967 election, in his efforts to discredit me, Bob voted against the Model Cities Program and even sent a letter to HUD Secretary Romney, objecting to the five-year plan. Curran did not run for reelection in 1971, although he remained in the area working in middle management at General Electric. He died in 2001.

Ralph Robinson: He was a reformer to the very end. As the Citizen County Legislator, he raised hell with the O'Connell machine. Not only was he a good fundraiser but also as Chairman of the Planning Commission, he provided the leadership to create a comprehensive plan and modern development codes that were a prerequisite for other federal grants. After his successful career running his own business, Ralph retired in Florida, not far from where I lived. We would meet from time to time for dinner and talk politics. He passed away in 1999 at the age of seventy-nine.

Frank Landry: He was another true reformer and a meticulous lawyer who always met the test of the courts when he prepared the county board of elections petitions for our candidates. As the police court judge appointed by Dr. Jay, he always went by the book. Frank left public service in 1967 to start his own law firm. He died in December of 2017, at the age of ninety.

Bill Riley: He was a dedicated reformer till the day he resigned as Chairman of the Model City Agency, as Vice Chair of the Citizens Party, and as Chairman of the Recreation Commission, all in 1969. Bill oversaw the creation or restoration of six city parks and developed recreation programs to address the needs of all ages, from small children to seniors. He was the clerk of the works for the new fire station and the construction manager for the new city swimming pool and the restoration of the music hall. Cohoesiers owe him a lot for the green space they now enjoy in town. Bill eventually moved to suburban Albany and went to work for a regional hospital in their operations department. He retired there as chief engineer. Bill and I are still friends and play golf together twice a year. At eighty-six, he is and always has been a gentleman.

Stanton Ablett: He was the Machine's City Court Judge under Big Mike, but as our Corporation Counsel, he became a dedicated reformer and a key player in the implementation of our programs and projects, and even our fights with the Machine. Stanton was reappointed Corporation Counsel after Curran's failed attempt to install Paul Coughlin, but after another two years, he retired. Stanton died in 1979.

Frank Bourgeois: He was a reformer who gained statewide recognition for his overhaul of the Cohoes Civil Service Commission, which became a model for other cities and towns in New York State. After Virginia's political crusade to get rid of him, Frank left the party, but not community service. After he retired from Mohawk Paper Mills as the Head of the Union, he moved across the river to Eagle Mills where he involved himself in various civic activities. I visited Frank shortly before he died in 2013 at the age of seventy-nine. We reminisced over his scrapbook of all the news articles citing his accomplishments as Civil Service Commissioner.

Albany *Times Union***:** Six years after I left Cohoes, I received a phone call in my office in Florida from a reporter at the *Times Union*. He said that the desks were missing from the Model Cities program. Since I had been director of the program, he wanted to know what had I done with them. After the initial shock of what he was implying, I thought to tell him that as I had only been director for one year and that during that time, we used four desks that belonged to the Cohoes Board of Education, where our offices were located. Also, it had been more than a decade since then. Then I thought better of it. Instead, I told the reporter to hang on, that I'd be just a moment. That was during a time when long distance phone calls were charged by the minute and were not cheap. I did not hang up but put the phone's handset on my desk and went back to work.

*The Troy Record***:** Fifty years after our 1963 election upset, I received a phone call from a reporter at the *Record*. She told me she was doing a story about our revolution. What she wrote, I am happy to say, turned out to be an accurate story. She even included the part about how her paper would not print any of our stories when we were a watchdog group.

City of Cohoes: The legacy of the Citizen Reform Movement is that after all these decades, our city has never returned to a "machine style" of politics or fears of corruption. Cohoesiers remain free to challenge their government without fear of reprisal, and the school district is free from political control. Its schools are updated, and their elected school board decide the governance most needed to improve the academic and social skills of our students and their future citizenship—our most valued legacy. However, since 1975, the city has had its ups and downs.

Mayor Canestrari, Virginia's successor, completed the fifth year of the Model Cities Program. His Commissioner of Public Works was indicted by a federal grand jury for taking bribes.

Mayor Signoracci, a successor, updated the comprehensive plan and initiated a waterfront redevelopment plan in which industrial relics were redeveloped into a new residential community. Mayor Signoracci's administration planned and received funding for redeveloping the corridor that ran through the mills in a historic content.

Then, Mayor John McDonald (no relation to Dr. Jay) supported private investment to convert the mills into upscale residential units.

Then, Mayor Morse implemented a facelift of the Cohoes Music Hall, a Model Cities Project and the city's cultural icon and initiated several improvement projects in the business district. However, Mayor Morse was indicted by a federal grand jury for embezzling party funds and was removed from office.

Unfortunately, all administrations have failed to maintain the City's infrastructure and function with many systems instituted fifty years ago. Recently, William Keeler, a retired Major from the New York State Police, was elected Mayor. He has the skills to raise the bar for better governance and to bring the city into the twenty-first century.

Reform and progress are what the citizen reformers worked and fought for so hard. And now, to realize that all these years later, they can proudly say that they helped create this force and founded our legacy—all the reward we ever wanted. Life is good.

Paul Van Buskirk: After leaving Cohoes, I moved to southwest Florida, where I have now lived for nearly forty years. It is a growing state, giving me plenty of opportunities as I established a planning firm. I consulted all along the East Coast and in Puerto Rico.

Over the years, I developed a copyrighted complex software tool, the Interactive Growth Model® (IGM), that accurately predicts when and where development takes place, and forecasts population demographics and needs for public facilities and commercial centers. This has allowed me to help communities, particularly those in the south, appropriately plan and manage growth, in order to optimize the rate of return on public capital investments. The IGM is the recipient of an American Planning Association Award and has been written up in Planning Magazine and trade journals for its application and accuracy.

I took time out to get my master's degree and Ph.D. in the behavioral sciences from Barry University in Miami. I have been a visiting lecturer at Yale University and the University of Florida, and an adjunct professor at Barry and Florida Gulf Coast Universities. I have written books, have coauthored several research papers, and am currently doing research on the relationship between school board governance and student performance.

I have a professional engineer license in three states and am a Charter Member of the American Planning Association and the American Institute of Certified Planners. More recently, I have been the recipient of the 2020 Distinguished Alumni Award from Barry University in Miami, Florida. Also in 2020 I was inducted to the American Institute of Certified Planners College of Fellows.

Over the years, my wife—Nancy—and I have traveled throughout Europe and the Caribbean. I am now in my eighties, still working, although not as much as before, since I have a golf game to perfect.

ACKNOWLEDGMENTS

This never-before-told story is the product of decades of my collecting documents, research, and testimony and newspaper accounts to provide a factual account of a story that needs to be told. I have been writing the manuscript for over the past five years. I have received the contribution of several people to provide an accurate account of events and content, which I call a team approach.

First, my contributing author, Whitney Fishburn, helped me organize my chapters and shared her journalistic and writing skills. Walter Lipka, city historian, shared with me his excellent research on the timeline of Big Mike. Charles Valenti, retired city planner, provided me with copies of the minutes of the Common Council, Board of Estimate and Apportionment, and the Board of Contract and Supply, as well as the official city elections results. Bill Riley and Harold Reavy provided their collection of documents and campaign paraphernalia.

Dave Bentley, Bill Riley, Charles Valenti, and Robert Signoracci reviewed the manuscript for content and accuracy. Dr. Mark Levine and his wife, Sally, analyzed each chapter and offered their recommendations for helping to maintain the book's flow and making it a page-turner.

My wife, Nancy, was supportive and patient as she proofread each chapter and let me use the dining table for my documents and my son, Michael for lending his computer skills. My development editor, David Ferris, offered his candid, talented review and recommendations for a smoother manuscript.

There were many talented people who successfully carried out many projects and dedicated their leadership to raise our city to the heights of an All-America City and a Model City. Some who provided leadership for our successful anti-poverty programs were:

Dorothy Miazga: Director of the Child Development Center; Faith Meyers Sandles: Director of the Senior Center and Rev. Gregory Weider, Rev. O'Brien; Larry Favreau: Director of the Neighborhood Youth Corps; and Robert Gullie: Director of the Cohoes Community Center.

For our Model City Program: Frank O'Connor, Urban Renewal Director, completed our urban project in forty-eight months, which was one of the few successful projects in the region. Andy Loiselle, despite his naiveté, and his assistant, Richard Shipman, completed one of the most difficult programs to rehabilitate acres of deteriorating mill housing and restore a neighborhood that is viable today. William Maloney, Director of the Human Resource Center and Barbara Shipman for consolidating the social services under one roof. Thomas Chmura, Assistant Director of Planning and Development for supporting me and aiding our projects during the war on all fronts.